FIVE STEPS OF OUTCOME-BASED PLANNING AND EVALUATION FOR PUBLIC LIBRARIES

MELISSA GROSS

CINDY MEDIAVILLA

VIRGINIA A. WALTER

<mark style="display:none">ala editions</mark>

AN IMPRINT OF THE AMERICAN LIBRARY ASSOCIATION

CHICAGO   2016

© 2016 by the American Library Association

Extensive effort has gone into ensuring the reliability of the information in this book; however, the publisher makes no warranty, express or implied, with respect to the material contained herein.

ISBNs
978-0-8389-1404-5 (paper)
978-0-8389-1415-1 (PDF)
978-0-8389-1416-8 (ePub)
978-0-8389-1417-5 (Kindle)

Library of Congress Cataloging-in-Publication Data

Names: Gross, Melissa, author. | Mediavilla, Cindy, 1953- author. | Walter, Virginia A., author.
Title: Five steps of outcome-based planning and evaluation for public libraries / Melissa Gross, Cindy Mediavilla, Virginia A. Walter.
Description: Chicago : ALA Editions, an imprint of the American Library Association, 2016. | Includes bibliographical references and index.
Identifiers: LCCN 2015043372| ISBN 9780838914045 (print : alk. paper) | ISBN 9780838914151 (pdf) | ISBN 9780838914168 (epub) | ISBN 9780838914175 (kindle)
Subjects: LCSH: Public libraries—Planning. | Public libraries—Evaluation. |Public services (Libraries)—Evaluation. | Libraries and community. | Public libraries—California—Planning—Case studies. | Public libraries—California—Evaluation—Case studies.
Classification: LCC Z678 .G74 2016 | DDC 027.4—dc23 LC record available at http://lccn .loc.gov/2015043372

Cover design by Alejandra Diaz. Text design in the Chaparral, Gotham, and Bell Gothic typefaces.

♾ This paper meets the requirements of ANSI/NISO Z39.48-1992 (Permanence of Paper).

Printed in the United States of America

20 19 18 17 16   5 4 3 2 1

Contents

Preface

IN 2013 WE CONDUCTED A SERIES OF WORKSHOPS throughout California on how to use the outcome-based planning and evaluation (OBPE) model to enhance and evaluate public library services. The training was a resounding success, with 99 percent of participants saying they now had a much better understanding of outcomes. As one participant enthused, "The presenters made what could've been a very confusing topic easy to understand and approachable. I feel like I can actually implement this without going crazy." Another described the workshop as "very important" because it helped attendees "look at the larger reasons for doing what we do." Inspired by these and other comments, the three of us looked at each other and decided, on the spot, to write this book.

Our goal here is to make the process accessible for readers interested in implementing OBPE in their projects. While other books have tackled the role of outcomes evaluation in libraries, no single volume exists on outcome-based planning and evaluation for public libraries—that is, until now. Our book targets public librarians, but should also be of use to library managers, grant writers, and anyone else developing, implementing, or evaluating new library programs and services for the public.

By the way, it wasn't long before we received requests for more training, and so an encore series of workshops was delivered in eight libraries across California in summer 2015. This time we added content on leveraging program results as the final step of the OBPE process. The workshops were again a huge success, with nearly 200 library staff members attending statewide. This book presents the same content delivered in our OBPE workshops.

Before proceeding, we do want to acknowledge several people and organizations in helping make this publication possible. First is the California State Library, which, through a Library Services and Technology Act grant administered by the Institute of Museum and Library Services (IMLS), made both series of workshops possible. We also want to thank IMLS for supporting the development of the original OBPE model through a demonstration and research grant. And finally, we thank all the workshop attendees, who, because of their overwhelming enthusiasm, inspired us to continue to hone the OBPE model and write this book.

MELISSA GROSS
CINDY MEDIAVILLA
VIRGINIA A. WALTER
August 2015

Introduction

MORE AND MORE, LIBRARIES ARE REQUIRED TO DEMONstrate their importance to stakeholders. Many libraries, like other organizations, engage in strategic planning in order to understand their community's information needs and to be aware of strengths, opportunities, weaknesses, and threats that can influence success. Evaluation is the process of understanding the extent to which specific goals are reached and provides information that is useful in demonstrating the library's worth. Evaluating library programs is also essential to continued planning. All of the activities related to strategic planning and evaluation take time, resources, training, and participation from all stakeholders to be performed well. If the process is too overwhelming, it becomes more difficult, if not impossible, for you to accomplish. Therefore, with this book, we have tried to make the process transparent and easy to follow. In our workshops, we urged people to start small and go step-by-step. We recommend that our readers do the same thing.

WHY OUTCOME-BASED EVALUATION?

There are many ways to evaluate library services. Among the most common is measuring inputs—that is, the resources you have and use to provide and support what you do. Inputs tend to be expressed numerically and capture the quantity of the various resources you use to provide service. Examples include numbers of librarians and staff, size of collections, amount of computers, and the library's physical infrastructure (e.g., square footage, number of meeting rooms, total seating, etc.). When describing your library in terms of inputs, you usually equate quality of service with the number of staff, books, computers, and so on that the library contains for its size. Your inputs might then be compared to professional standards or similarly sized institutions to determine how well your library is performing. The annual documentation of inputs allows you to track the library's performance year to year or conduct trend analysis over several years. However, an increase in resources, or even knowing the library has a wealth of resources, doesn't tell you much about the extent to which, how, or with what effect people use your services.

Consequently, the library field developed output measures that describe resource use. Beginning in the 1980s, a series of output measures books for public libraries was published by the American Library Association (ALA) and its divisions (Van House, Zweizig, and the Public Library Association New Standards Task Force 1987; Zweizig and Rodger 1982; Walter 1992; Walter 1995). Outputs were later incorporated into measuring the needs of networked public libraries (Bertot, McClure, and Ryan 2000) and into the evaluation of digital reference services (McClure, Lankes, Gross, and Choltco-Devlin 2002).

Output measures typically focus on "how much" or "how many" of the library's resources are used. An output measure collected by most libraries is circulation—that is, the extent to which materials are being checked out. Circulation statistics tell us how often items are checked out, and for how long, and are typically used to determine library funding. Other common output measures include program attendance and reference transaction counts. When program attendance is strong, and maybe even growing over time, you usually take this as a sign of success. Likewise, you might track the number of reference transactions to determine usage patterns, so you can schedule the reference desk accordingly.

Input and output measures provide useful data, but they don't tell us how library programs benefit participants. Neither do they tell us anything about user satisfaction or what the library means in the lives of the people it serves. Therefore, the Institute of Museum and Library Services (IMLS) began to look for additional ways to evaluate and talk about programs and services in terms of their impact on people's lives. Though it may be good to know that 100 community members attended a lecture at the library, it also helps to know what effect the lecture had on its audience. Did the lecture help make them better citizens, more literate, more employable, happier? Outcome measures are designed to support evaluation that gets at the human experience and allows you to use the voices of participants to talk about the merits, as well as the shortcomings, of that experience. While outcomes may be used in conjunction with inputs and outputs, they differ from them fundamentally in that outcomes focus on human impact, which is often described through the participants' own words. Not only does this feedback tell you how effective your services are, but it can also be used to make program improvements, to terminate programs that aren't working, and to help you design new programs.

Despite universal acknowledgment that outcomes are now the de facto method for measuring the effectiveness of library programs, staff and managers don't necessarily know how to use outcomes to plan and evaluate services. Moreover, previous outcome-based planning models have been deemed too complicated to use. The Outcome-Based Planning and Evaluation (OBPE) process tested as part of the CATE (Children's Access to and Use of Technology Evaluation) Project provides a comprehensive and comprehensible model that has been demonstrated in public libraries by a variety of target user groups. Our book walks you through, step-by-step, the OBPE model in designing and implementing library programs and services.

DEVELOPMENT OF THE OBPE MODEL

Developed by the Florida State University College of Information and the St. Louis Public Library and supported by an IMLS demonstration research grant, the CATE Project used OBPE to plan, design, develop, and evaluate technology programs for youth ages 8 to 13. The project was revolutionary in that it was among the first studies to look at how youth actually use computers in the library. In addition, the children themselves, along with other stakeholders in the community, helped determine the outcomes the technology programs were designed to achieve. The results of the project were published by ALA as *Dynamic Youth Services through Outcome-Based Planning and Evaluation* (Dresang, Gross, and Holt 2006) and have been used to assess services and programs in public libraries. OBPE has also provided the basis for countless workshops at professional conferences and individual library systems. Indeed, the success of these workshops is the reason we wrote this book!

HOW TO USE THIS BOOK

Our book builds on the four-step CATE OBPE model and extends it to public librarians serving the entire community. We have also extended the original OBPE model by adding a fifth step on how to use outcomes to increase library visibility in the community. Although our primary audience is public librarians, we have found that library managers, grant writers, and anyone developing, implementing or evaluating new library services can also benefit from OBPE. Among the concepts explored in this book are:

> **Defining "outcomes"**—What they are and why public librarians should use them to plan and evaluate services.
>
> **Assessing the community**—The rationale behind and methodologies for assessing community needs and interests that will then inform the creation of new library programs

and services. Methods include key informant interviews, surveys, focus groups, and environmental scans.

Determining outcomes—How to use community assessment data to create outcome statements that not only guide the creation of new library services, but also provide targets for measuring the effectiveness of those services.

Developing programs and services—How to design services that directly relate to the community's needs and interests, while achieving the outcomes the library has targeted.

Evaluating programs and services—How to use outcome statements to design and conduct an evaluation plan that measures the effectiveness of the library's new services.

Sharing results—How to maximize the results of successful outcome-based programs to leverage the library's role in the community.

Each area above is addressed in a separate chapter, followed by a set of appendixes that offer sample data-gathering instruments to be used during the community assessment step of the OBPE process. There is also a bibliography of related resources for further reading.

If you are new to OBPE, chapter 1 will orient you to important terminology and the five-step model. Chapters 2 through 6 contain specific information and advice related to each step and may be used by both new and experienced managers as they advance in designing, developing, implementing, and evaluating projects. Chapter 2 discusses how to perform an assessment in order to understand the needs and aspirations of your community in a way that supports planning. Chapter 3 helps you use community assessment data in targeting outcomes to respond to user information needs. Chapter 4 provides advice on the process of program development, and chapter 5 walks you through how to evaluate whether your project helped users attain the outcomes it was designed to deliver. Chapter 6 gives advice about sharing your results with various stakeholder groups and how to make sure the community knows how your library is contributing to its well-being. All of the chapters provide examples of how to proceed through each phase of the OBPE model.

Whatever size your project, we believe OBPE can help you and your library attain your program and service goals. We would be happy to hear how you use the OBPE model and how it has impacted your library and the community.

REFERENCES

Bertot, John, Charles R. McClure, and Joe Ryan. 2000. *Statistics and Performance Measures for Public Library Networked Services.* Chicago: American Library Association.

Dresang, Eliza T., Melissa Gross, and Leslie E. Holt. 2006. *Dynamic Youth Services through Outcome-Based Planning and Evaluation.* Chicago: American Library Association.

McClure, Charles R., David R. Lankes, Melissa Gross, and Beverly Choltco-Devlin. 2002. *Statistics, Measures, and Quality Standards for Assessing Digital Reference Library Services: Guidelines and Procedures.* Syracuse, NY: Information Institute of Syracuse, School of Information Studies, Syracuse University; and Tallahassee, FL: School of Information Studies, Information Use Management and Policy Institute, Florida State University. quartz.syr.edu/rdlankes/Publications/Books/Quality.pdf.

Van House, Nancy, et al. 1987. *Output Measures for Public Libraries: A Manual of Standardized Procedures.* 2nd ed. Chicago: American Library Association.

Walter, Virginia A. 1995. *Output Measures and More: Planning and Evaluating Public Library Services for Young Adults.* Chicago: American Library Association.

———. 1992. *Output Measures for Public Library Service to Children: A Manual of Standardized Procedures.* Chicago: American Library Association.

Zweizig, Douglas, and Eleanor Jo Rodger. 1982. *Output Measures for Public Libraries: A Manual of Standardized Procedures.* Chicago: American Library Association.

1

Outcomes, Services and Programs, and OBPE

OUTCOME-BASED PLANNING AND EVALUATION (OBPE) explains how to integrate an outcome-based orientation into the library's regular planning and evaluation cycles. It can be used with any size project and, when applied to strategic planning, ensures that

- Goals and objectives target the kind of outcomes the community wants to experience as a result of library use
- Planning and program development are data-driven
- Evaluation is integrated from the beginning of the development process

The OBPE model is a series of steps, or "phases," that naturally lead into each other. This chapter discusses the important terms that are central to OBPE and provides a general overview of the individual steps that make up the model.

BEGIN BY UNDERSTANDING WHAT
YOU WANT TO ACHIEVE

The key to any type of evaluation is to know, from the start, what you are trying to achieve. For example, think about employee performance. Whether you are the person evaluating an employee or the employee who is being evaluated, it is important to know what the organization's performance expectations are. These expectations may derive from the position description, professional standards, the mission and goals of the library, or a combination of all of the above. Agreeing in advance which competencies, standards, or goals will be used to assess an employee's performance makes evaluation understandable to all the parties involved. This also lets individuals know how outstanding performance is defined and provides guidance for any needed improvement. The same is true for assessing library programs and services.

Library *services* are the ways in which the library makes its resources available to users (Reitz 2014). Examples include availability of materials, provision of electronic resources, reference help and mediated searching, and interlibrary loan. Public library services may also be defined according to user group, as in adult or children's services. While it is not unusual for people to conflate the terms *services* and *programs*, *programs* are differentiated as "an activity or event (or series of events) scheduled by a library for the benefit of its patrons" (Reitz 2014). Examples of programs include book clubs, résumé help, computer-training workshops, or events held to reach specific populations in the community. Services and programs can be thought of in terms of the kind of impact (i.e., outcomes) we want participants to experience as a result of their library use.

Designing new services provides an opportunity to initiate the OBPE model to ensure that program planning, development, and evaluation are focused on desired user outcomes. Existing services and programs can also be reexamined and revised, if needed, to incorporate target outcomes as part of the normal ongoing planning and evaluation process. But we want to warn against looking for service and program outcomes in an ad hoc or rearview mirror fashion. Assigning outcomes, after the fact, cannot guarantee that services and programs will respond to community needs or provide coherent data for future planning. Imagine how disturbing it would be for an employee to be evaluated according to surprise performance criteria, regardless of whether the ultimate outcome was positive or negative!

WHAT ARE OUTCOMES?

The IMLS defines *outcomes* as "benefits to people"—that is, the positive changes in one's "skill, knowledge, attitude, behavior, condition, or life status" (Institute of Museum and Library Services n.d.). Outcomes measure the impact that services and programs have on their target populations. When properly used, outcomes can guide and help evaluate the effectiveness of the programs and services a library provides. As retired Texas State Library director Peggy Rudd once posited, outcomes have "the potential to be a powerful tool to help us substantiate the claims we know to be true about the impact of libraries in our institutions and in our society" (Rudd n.d.). So what does it mean to change a person's skill, knowledge, attitude, behavior, condition, or life status?

Skill

A change in skill results from learning to do something you weren't able to do before or improving performance in an area where you already had some ability. Typical skills encountered in libraries include reading, trouble-shooting technology, finding information, and critical thinking. A skill-based program focuses on teaching people a skill they lack or need—for example, a basic literacy service that teaches adults how to read. Skill-based programs can also assist people in improving a skill they already have—for example, helping users go from a beginner to an intermediate level when searching the Internet.

Knowledge

A change in knowledge leads to gaining or expanding command of a subject area. This could result in acquiring all kinds of data, including learning about facts, statistics, events, theories, literatures, cultures, and more. Changes in knowledge can come from education, personal experience, or learning from the experiences of others. Examples of library programs that seek to increase knowledge include lectures on local history, presentations on genealogical resources, and book clubs.

Attitude

A change in attitude involves ways of thinking or feeling. Library programs focused on an attitude-based outcome are designed to change opinions or dispositions or a person's orientation towards a topic, institution, or activity. When you offer programs that promote reading as being fun or show that recycling is beneficial for all, you are hoping to affect attitude.

Behavior

A change in behavior means affecting what people do. Programs that aim to change behaviors are focused on actions, working either to promote or inhibit certain kinds of activities. Examples include programs that seek to encourage people to vote, spend more time reading, or learn how to protect their privacy online.

Condition or Status

A change in condition or status involves helping people improve social, professional, or other aspects of their personal circumstance. Some examples of library programs aimed at this kind of change are those that help improve a person's life condition or transform perceptions of participants as readers, computer users, employed people, or citizens.

THE OBPE MODEL

As described above, OBPE is a process in which library services and programs are intentionally designed to impact people in specific ways. Impacts are defined as outcomes that will improve the lives of library users by helping them obtain desired skills or knowledge, attitudes or behaviors, or make improvements in their condition or status. The OBPE process works to develop outcome goals that are consistent with community needs, the library's mission, and stakeholder opinions. The model can be used to guide any library project, large or small. However, we recommend starting small to see how the steps fit together before using the process to plan and evaluate a larger program.

The OBPE model is comprised of five phases that feed into each other. What's learned along the way can be used to improve future planning, service and program development, evaluation, and how to effectively leverage the library's role in the community. The cyclical nature of OBPE ensures that projects are in sync with library planning and rooted in an understanding of the population being served. Outcomes are generated based on data and then integrated into service and program criteria. Strategies for evaluating library activities are also determined during the development phase and are designed to measure targeted outcomes. Services and programs are assessed and findings are used to further improve library activities, inform future planning, and are shared with stakeholders. The feedback received from stakeholders then becomes part of the market research used to inform continued planning and project development. A flow chart of the OBPE process is represented in figure 1.1.

PHASE I
Gathering Information

The best place to start working on any program or service is with a firm grounding in information. It is important to understand your library's mission, policies, and strategic plan so you and others can

FIGURE 1.1

Outcome-Based Planning and Evaluation Model

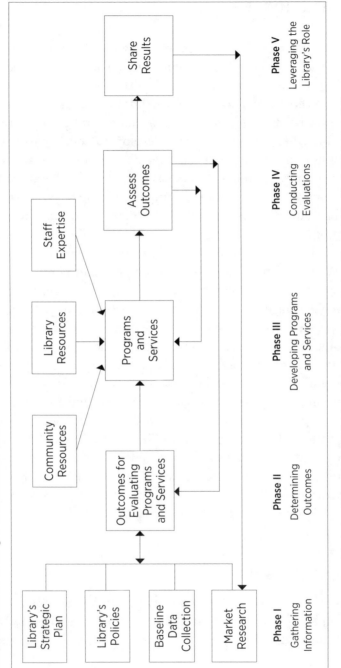

This model is an extension of the Project CATE OBPE Model developed as part of an IMLS Research and Demonstration Grant. See Dresang, E. T., Gross, M., & Holt, L. E. (2006). *Dynamic Youth Services through Outcome-Based Planning and Evaluation*. Chicago, IL: ALA Editions, p. xi.

see how your efforts contribute to the overall goals and objectives of the organization. It is equally important to understand the community the library is meant to serve, as well as the specific audience being targeted. For example, you may consider competing for a grant that will support services to older adults. To get the grant, you must demonstrate not only that such a service is needed, but also that the library is the right organization to provide the service. Questions to ask yourself as you prepare the grant application:

- Is service to older adults consistent with the library's mission, goals, and objectives?
- To what extent is the library already responding to this community and with what kind of success?
- Which other organizations in the community already serve this user group?
- What is known about older adults in the community (marital status, economic status, ethnicity, gender, education levels, etc.)?
- What is known about older adults' information needs, preferred sources, access to technology, and literacies (computer, communication technologies, etc.)?

Some of this information will be available in the library or through published resources, either in print or on the web. Use these sources first, before contacting experts to help fill in the gaps. Details on gathering information to support outcome-based planning and evaluation are provided in chapter 2, "Gathering Information."

PHASE II
Determining Outcomes

As you read and review the data collected in Phase I, you'll begin to see patterns that indicate what's important to your target audience—for example, what would older adults like to achieve with the help of the library? Your analysis will no doubt reveal:

- Where service and program needs are in the community
- How the library can best serve the target group's needs
- Whether you need to collect more data if analysis reveals new questions
- What kind of outcomes should be targeted in developing services or programs for this population
- Indicators that can be used to determine whether targeted outcomes have been achieved

Let's assume Phase I reveals a popular interest in genealogy among local older adults. Happily, this aligns with the library's mission to support the intellectual and recreational information needs of the overall community. Data collected from various sources, including the adults themselves, are analyzed to determine which type of outcome(s) would best be served—for example, a desire for increased *knowledge* of genealogical resources or perhaps a need to improve research *skills*. Once the types of possible outcomes are identified, you then consider how to state and measure achievement of the outcome(s). So, for the outcome of improving skills in conducting genealogical research, a one-sentence description might be "to increase older adults' ability to research family history." An indicator of outcome achievement might be that 50 percent of the older adults participating in the library's genealogy program will be able to complete their family tree. Further details on Phase II are provided in chapter 3, "Determining Outcomes."

PHASE III
Developing Programs and Services

For many of us, the fun part of OBPE is designing the program or service to achieve the outcome designated in Phase II. Indeed, most library staff are experts at planning and carrying out programs. But don't forget to think about evaluation and how you intend to measure the success of your project. There are many ways to help improve the genealogy research skills of older adults. Teaching participants how to search appropriate resources might involve local historical or special collections, accessing specific databases, or learning to search the Internet more effectively. Assessing participants' ability to successfully access genealogical resources can be used to evaluate your program as long as you consider, in advance, how to demonstrate the impact of participation on the user's skill. Improved skill can usually be evaluated through observation, testing, or by asking participants to describe what they've learned.

When initiating any new project, it is important to understand what resources are available to support the design, development, evaluation, and sustainability of your program or service. In Phase III, you will consider what resources are available within the library, as well as in the local community, to help implement your new service or program. You must also assess whether existing staff have the expertise to successfully carry out the project and whether extra personnel are needed. Determining these factors ahead of time will help shape your program accordingly. Details on how to design outcome-based projects are provided in chapter 4, "Designing Programs and Services."

PHASE IV
Conducting Evaluations

Evaluation lets you know whether your program or service is delivering the outcome(s) it was designed to achieve. If goals aren't being reached, then evaluation can help inform you on how to improve services and programs to make them more effective or efficient. Outcome-based programs must be routinely assessed to make sure they are still relevant, of high quality, and responsive to the community's needs. In OBPE, evaluation is used to document success, improve performance, and plan for the future. Therefore, Phase IV is connected to all of the other phases in the model. Not only are current program results used to improve service design and delivery, but evaluation data may also inform decisions about the types of outcomes selected for further program improvement or development. Chapter 5, "Evaluating Programs and Services," will orient you to the issues and processes related to evaluation.

PHASE V
Leveraging the Library's Role

Once you have delivered and assessed your outcome-based program, you will want to share your accomplishments with others. Use participants' own words to describe how the program impacted their lives. Regaining a lost personal history or documenting family stories may be wonderful by-products of the genealogy research program. In addition, older adults may have improved their research skills, while enjoying a fun but meaningful leisure activity. It is imperative that the results of successful programs be communicated to library staff, the community in general, and the specific stakeholders who are interested in promoting the library. You will want everyone to know how the library is using outcome-based planning and evaluation to connect with, support, and respond to the information and recreational needs of the community. Sharing the positive outcomes of your work helps to demonstrate the centrality of the library in the life of the community and promotes good will. The results of your project may even help build continued support for library funding.

In every project there will be successes as well as lessons learned. In fact, the OBPE process is completely iterative. Not only does evaluation reveal ways to improve what you are doing, it also provides ideas for future services and programs and uncovers new outcomes to be targeted. Details on how to use outcomes to leverage the library's role in the community are discussed in chapter 6, "Sharing Results."

BENEFITS OF OBPE IN THE PUBLIC LIBRARY

The use of outcome-based evaluation has become standard for many organizations and is routinely required by funding agencies. However, understanding the process may not be enough for its successful use. The model is most robust when it is implemented continuously and utilizes feedback that connects the use of evaluation data to service improvements, outreach efforts, and future planning. Input must be solicited from both inside and outside the library. Services developed without community feedback are unlikely to have the same relevance and impact as those that include user input in all phases of the model. Without this input, you will have a more difficult time demonstrating that the library is interested in and responsive to its community.

Now, you may be thinking this process sounds engaging, but really, is it worth all the trouble? Why not just develop services with an "if we build it, they will come" attitude? We, of course, are convinced that it *is* worth the time and effort to intentionally develop services by anticipating user impact. Not only does OBPE prevent wasted time and effort, it also improves program success rates.

Responds to Community Needs

Being responsive to community needs and interests is central to the library's ability to place itself at the heart of community life. By asking non-users and users alike what is needed to help them improve their daily lives, you not only demonstrate a desire to respond to constituents' needs, you also gain important information on how to meet those needs and aspirations. This may lead you to rethink old services and programs as well as systematically initiate new ones. OBPE places primary focus on the community, not on the library.

Improves Library Management

With its emphasis on planning, OBPE helps you make good managerial decisions by ensuring that limited resources are employed in the most effective manner. Over time, the use of OBPE helps build staff capacity to be reflective, effective, and intentional practitioners. Furthermore, the process motivates staff to support the library's mission and goals and to continue to be informed about the community they serve.

Provides Important Data

Data on user impact are increasingly required from funders. Systematically collecting and using data in planning, service development, and evaluation ensures that evidence of achievement is consistently available for internal use as well as for seeking funding. Being able to articulate the role of the library in community life is essential in building and maintaining stakeholder relationships.

Helps Promote the Library

Finally, OBPE answers the question *"so what?"* To us, the library's importance to society is obvious, but you may be increasingly called upon to explain the library's role and substantiate why it should be supported. OBPE provides concrete, evidence-based data regarding the impact of library services on individuals and community life and ensures that you are making these impacts known.

CHALLENGES IN ADOPTING OBPE

We hope we have made the benefits of OBPE clear. After exploring each step in the following chapters, we are confident you will see how the OBPE framework can be incorporated into your library's planning cycle. Still, as with anything else that's new, challenges will arise. In particular, people may be resistant to the changes OBPE represents. This is a common reaction when asked to try something new or do things in a different way. Another challenge may be the perception that the process adds an unnecessary added workload. While we acknowledge that OBPE can add to one's workload, we are convinced the process is necessary to maintaining the library's relevance to its community. We hope staff will learn to appreciate OBPE once they see how it validates their role in the community.

Lack of administrative support may present another type of challenge. Ideally, program development is easier to do when staff and administration agree on the best way to accomplish the library's goals and objectives. Just as personnel need to understand how OBPE benefits them in their work, library administrators may need to become aware (if they aren't already) that outcome-based evaluation has been widely adopted by government and other public service agencies. Undertaking a demonstration project may make the benefits of OBPE clear. Starting with a small project will allow you to demonstrate the OBPE process and how outcomes can be leveraged to increase the visibility of the library and its importance in the life of its users.

Finally, you may feel like there is an awful lot to know regarding OBPE. This may be especially true of the evaluation phase. The extent to which new skills are needed will depend on whether the OBPE process is already a regular part of the library's procedures. Consider what outcomes the library needs to meet to establish an OBPE culture and make it successful. Do staff need to experience a positive change in knowledge, skills, behaviors, or attitudes to support OBPE implementation? It may be useful to start with a small project and build needed expertise through training. Confidence will build as additional programs and services are added. Staff may also find that their job satisfaction has grown. After all, OBPE ensures that the library is responsive to the community. Being able to demonstrate success is a powerful way to express the library's importance to all stakeholders!

REFERENCES

Institute of Museum and Library Services. "Outcome Based Evaluations." www.imls.gov/grants/outcome-based-evaluations.

Reitz, Joan M. 2014. "Online Dictionary for Library and Information Science (ODLIS)." www.abc-clio.com/ODLIS/odlis_A.aspx.

Rudd, Peggy D. "Documenting the Difference: Demonstrating the Value of Libraries Through Outcome Measurement." In *Perspectives on Outcome-Based Evaluation for Libraries and Museums,* 16–23. Washington, DC: Institute of Museum and Library Services. www.imls.gov/assets/1/workflow_staging/AssetManager/perspectivesobe.pdf.

2

Gathering Information

YOU HAVE NOW BEEN INTRODUCED TO THE OUTCOME-based planning and evaluation logic model. We have found that using this five-step approach is an effective and convenient way for public libraries to involve staff, volunteers, and stakeholders in their planning and evaluation efforts. In this chapter, we will provide you with strategies for implementing Phase I, "Gathering Information," with an emphasis on assessing the community.

The previous chapter outlined many of the benefits of using an outcome-based approach to planning and evaluation. In addition, there are some specific benefits that result from the community assessment phase of the process. A good community assessment brings into focus both subtle and dramatic changes in your service area. Have you noticed fewer older adults and more young families using the library? Why? Perhaps the older adults are selling their larger homes in order to move into smaller condos or assisted living residences, and young families are snapping them up. Are schools responding to this change in meaningful ways? How does this suggest changes in your library's collections and services? A community assessment should take you and your staff out of the library's walls and into the neighborhoods you serve. This will increase the visibility of the library as well as its credibility as an institution that cares about extending its reach. The community assessment process will help you identify competitors and potential partners, facilitating future outreach efforts for your library.

Although your assessment will involve some basic research methods you may remember from library school, we will give you a brief refresher course here. You'll be undertaking a form of action research that's intended to result in practical action-oriented outcomes.

LIBRARY'S STRATEGIC PLAN AND POLICIES

The OBPE model (figure 1.1) suggests four areas for gathering information. Now is the time to review the library's existing strategic plan and policies that might affect the priorities, programs, and services you decide to pursue as a result of this planning process. There may not be a current strategic plan, but almost all public libraries have created a mission statement you can refer to. These tend to be quite general, allowing a great deal of latitude in interpretation. For example, the Santa Monica Public Library (SMPL) has crafted the following mission statement: "To provide resources, services, and a place to encourage the community to Read, Connect, Relax, and Learn" (Santa Monica Public Library Mission and Vision n.d.). This wide-ranging mission leaves room to develop recreational and community-building services, in addition to more traditional educational resources and reading promotion schemes.

More specific hints about the library's culture can be found in its published policies (Santa Monica Public Library Policies n.d.). Policies for dealing with such issues as service animals, Internet use, filming, and rules of conduct are outlined in some detail. A closer look at the rules of conduct indicates a number of prohibited activities that reflect the library's location in a beach community and as a magnet for homeless adults. Library patrons are reminded not to use the restrooms for bathing, shaving, or washing hair and clothing. On the other hand, a person can be asked to leave if one's bodily hygiene is offensive and a nuisance to others. Library patrons are expected to wear shoes, shirts, and appropriate outer clothing.

The SMPL's existing policies would suggest that if subsequent research into community demographics indicated the need for recreational or educational services for its homeless population, care would have to be taken to do so in ways that were sensitive to the needs of people without the basic resources for personal hygiene or safety. This might indicate the desirability of forming partnerships with social service and mental health organizations. It might also indicate a need for staff training in handling delicate interpersonal encounters with street people.

In our appendixes, we have included a useful form, called "Community Assessment Environmental Scan: Internal (Library) Factors" (appendix A), to help you organize data about the library's resources as well as its mission, history, and culture. The scan will also help assess whether the library has the capacity to take on a new program or service. After you have gathered this internal information, the OBPE team should meet and discuss the implications of your findings.

BASELINE DATA COLLECTION

Relevant Phase I baseline data include those statistics that relate to library usage, such as circulation, reference tallies, door count, computer usage, and program attendance. Make these figures available to your OBPE team and discuss the implications of what you see. What part of the collection gets the most use? Has circulation increased or gone down recently? What accounts for the increase and decrease in door count at various times of the day? Who is using the public access computers? Is attendance at programs, such as toddler storytime or the adult book club, consistent or does it vary with the seasons?

You may find it useful to compare your library's statistics (e.g., collection size and circulation) with those of other libraries of comparable size. The *Public Library Data Service*, available by subscription from the Public Library Association, provides annual data on staffing, operating finances, output measures, interlibrary loans, and technology provisions from 1,100 North American libraries of various sizes. Each year there is also a special section focusing on a particular service area or public library topic. In 2013, for example, a special survey presented data on outcome measures. This is also a good time to think about missing data. Is there some aspect of library usage that you have failed to account for? How might you collect these data in the future?

MARKET RESEARCH

Our OBPE logic model calls the next data-gathering element of Phase I, "Market Research." This is the term commonly used in private business. Some strategic plans also call this an "environmental scan." We like to think of this as a community assessment, designed to help library staff understand the needs, assets, and aspirations of the people they serve. Before you begin to conduct your community assessment, you need to make three key decisions. The first is to define the scope of your effort. While community assessments are an essential part of any planning initiative, those undertaken as part of OBPE tend to be limited to a target community, population, or service. A grant proposal, for example, often requires evidence of a needs assessment. An early childhood literacy proposal would involve very different data collection than one dealing with enhanced information services for small businesses or book clubs for older adults.

The second decision is to determine the level of effort to be expended on the assessment phase. Our own experience as consultants has been that greater effort at this stage pays off in many ways.

Getting out into the community to gather information brings visibility to your planning effort and helps you identify potential partners. It facilitates future outreach, and it helps you track the subtle changes in your community as well as the more obvious and dramatic ones. However, as we observed in chapter 1, there may be staff resistance to the OBPE initiative, as a whole and to this step in particular, and there may be good reasons to streamline your community data collection. We'll suggest a variety of methods involving various levels of effort in the next section.

The third decision you need to make is the composition of your assessment team. We recommend that you consider involving community members as part of your assessment team. They bring a particular perspective that is a good counterpoint to that of professional librarians. Karen Hacker (2013, 5) describes the joining together of local and professional knowledge as "street science," a term coined by Jason Corburn. Members of the community acquire local knowledge through their own experiences, interpersonal communication, and cultural tradition. Professionals, on the other hand, acquire their specialized knowledge through education and systematic data collection and research. Local knowledge is deemed credible through the evidence of one's own eyes and experience, while professionals tend to rely on statistical significance and legal standards. Local knowledge is tested and presented in public narratives and community stories, while professional knowledge achieves credibility through peer review, courts, and the media. The best community assessments bring together both frameworks for seeing the world.

HOW TO DO IT: METHODS FOR COLLECTING COMMUNITY INFORMATION AND DATA

Informal Information Sharing/Brainstorming

The least time-intensive way to conduct a community needs assessment is through informal information sharing and brainstorming. This is the approach the Los Angeles Public Library (LAPL) successfully used the first year it participated in California's new out-come- and outreach-based summer reading program initiative. Informal information sharing is a way to tap into the collective knowledge and understanding of the library staff about the community. This is how you do it: Schedule a staff meeting for at least one hour in the morning, if at all possible. Bring munchies and drinks and be sure that *all* staff attend. Some of these people probably live in the community and will have a very different perspective from those who commute from other areas.

Start by going around the table and asking each person to make one statement that describes what's going on in the community. Some possible responses could be:

"People are worried about gang activity."

"Traffic is getting worse every day."

"There is no place to buy fresh fruit and vegetables."

"That apartment building on 25th Street is now completely rented by Somalis."

"There is a new housing development going up along Route 15."

"Summer school is canceled this year."

"There are some great new restaurants opening up on Main Street."

"Teachers are gearing up for Common Core next fall."

Then move on to a more focused look at the community, based on the particular purpose for your needs assessment. The LAPL needed to find a streamlined, but informed, method for each branch library to use to identify targets for their summer reading programs. Young adult and children's librarians conducted the staff meetings. Participants were asked to share their insights into the lives of families, children, and teens during the summer months. Were summer readers looking for recreational or educational opportunities? What services or programs were other agencies providing? Had there been any demographic changes in the neighborhood recently? Any redevelopment efforts? Based on this discussion, staff identified one underserved element in their community on which to focus their summer outreach efforts. These conversations led to decisions about where to focus their outreach efforts. An unintended positive consequence was an unusually strong buy-in, from the whole staff, to the extra workload that is an inevitable by-product of summer reading programs.

Data Mining

Information scientists talk a lot about data mining. This refers to any of a number of strategies for extracting useful information from databases. For our purposes, let's think of this as locating relevant information from recorded or published sources. If you haven't looked at the most recent census data for your service area, you should do this now. The census provides an invaluable source of information about demographic data, such as income levels, household size, ethnicity, and other topics. There are many other online resources that may be useful to you. And don't forget state and local databases that are specific to your location. Many state education departments, for example, compile important and relevant statistics about graduation rates, reading and math scores, and ethnicity for school districts and sometimes even individual schools. Our form, called "Community Assessment Environmental Scan: External (Community) Factors" (appendix B), is a handy place to start compiling these data.

Other sources of relevant information include published or online directories, produced by local government agencies, elected officials, chambers of commerce, and community service organizations. Even the old-fashioned telephone directory, in its traditional print or new electronic format, is a useful resource for identifying potential partners or leads for more in-depth information about a particular area of interest. Depending on your focus, you may want to begin to compile your own list of relevant agencies, organizations, and individuals. Some of these might include:

- Educational programs, including public and independent schools, tutoring programs, preschools, and home schooling organizations

- Colleges and universities, especially those with academic specializations pertinent to your program
- Local government: elected officials and representatives from relevant city and county departments
- Health and human service agencies: WIC (women, infants, and children) programs, halfway houses, senior citizen centers, homeless shelters, juvenile detention facilities, and recreation centers
- Clubs: 4H, Scouts, Boys and Girls Clubs, garden clubs, and service clubs, such as Kiwanis and Rotary
- Civic organizations
- Religious organizations
- Business groups
- Recreational services: playgrounds, golf courses, tennis courts, and skate parks
- Cultural resources: museums, drama programs, mural programs, music, dance, or art classes and performance venues
- Ethnic organizations

When you have extracted as much information as you can from existing data sources, it is time to move on to the next two methods of community assessment: field research and questioning people directly through interviews, focus groups, or surveys.

Field Research

Up to this point, you could have done all your community assessment work sitting at your desk or in a meeting room in your library. Now it's time to get out into the field and immerse yourself in the community. Think of this as research by walking around. Actually, you can conduct the first and easiest field research from your car, bicycle, or bus seat on your way to work. Try taking different routes and pay attention to what you see. Get out of the building and drive or walk around at different times of the day. Observe how people get around. Is this a walking community? Who rides the bus? Look, too, for places where people congregate and where they shop. What do they do for fun? Notice the languages used on signs and whether businesses are opening or closing. What employment opportunities exist? Appendix C, "Community Assessment: Field Questions to Ask Yourself," provides a checklist of questions to ask yourself when conducting your field research.

After you've taken your commuter tour, it's time to really get out and walk. Wear or carry something that identifies you as a library employee: a T-shirt or tote bag will do. Eat lunch at different venues. Make a point to shop at local stores. Introduce yourself to employees and customers everywhere. Engage them in conversation. Invite them to come visit you at the library. Leave flyers and bookmarks. Sharpen your observation skills, while you're out and about and mingling with the residents in the community.

Much of this initial field research gives you a kind of background or landscape view of your community. Now you need to zero in on the aspects of your community that are most relevant to your outcome-based plan. Go back to your data mining results. You should have compiled a list of the community assets most relevant to your project. Start with the agency or organization that is most likely to be useful to you. It might be the senior citizen center or Head Start that is closest to the library. Make an appointment to meet with their director or visit a staff meeting. Have a conversation about what they are trying to achieve and what they see happening in the community. Tell them about your proposed project and get their feedback. Ask them to refer you to other people in the community who might be helpful. Keep track of names and contact information, as these will be helpful later on if you decide to interview key informants or develop partnerships.

Asking Questions

The people who live and work in the community your library serves are going to be your best and most useful sources of information. Any thorough community needs assessment will tap into their expertise. You just need to find a good way to ask them the right questions. (See appendix D, "Community Assessment: Sample Interview and Focus Group Questions," for a list of sample interview and focus group questions.) The methods that social scientists and marketing specialists use for this purpose are interviews, focus groups, and surveys.

Interviews

Interviews are often the primary source of data in the kind of action research you are conducting for your community assessment. You will want to talk with key informants—that is, people who are the most pertinent sources of local knowledge—and key stakeholders—the people most likely to be affected by the services or programs you'll design as a result of your research. Some of these people were no doubt identified during the data mining and field research phases discussed above. There is no magic number of interviewees, but you will want to talk to enough people to give you a fair and unbiased overview of the issues and topics of concern.

In his guide to action research, Ernest T. Stringer (2014, 104ff.) suggests that you characterize interviews as informal conversations when you approach a potential participant. You might approach the president of the local chamber of commerce like this: "I'd like to talk with you about how you see things going for small businesses in our community. When could we have a conversation?" You want to create a situation in which your interviewees feel comfortable and will be most likely to tell you what they are really thinking. You also want to interview participants to explore the topic in their own terms. Try to avoid phrasing your questions in terms of what the library might do. Instead, encourage people to talk about their own experiences. Action researchers have developed a sequence of questioning that seems to bring this out.

Start with very general questions: "I'm trying to learn more about the small business community here. What can you tell me about it?" "I don't know very much about teenagers here. What are your insights about life for teens here?" You can then move on to typical questions that encourage your respondents to tell you how things usually work or happen: "How do most small businesses get started here?" "What do the teens you know plan to do after they graduate from high school?" Finally, ask specific questions that focus on specific events or situations: "How did local businesses respond to the new Walmart going in?" "What happens at the after-school tutoring sessions?" You may extend the answers by asking for more information and by encouraging people to tell you more or to give you an example. Ask them what they think is needed to help address the issues under discussion. Think about potential outcomes. How do people describe their current situation? What would they like the future to bring?

Most people want to know that the interviewer is paying attention and really hearing what they have to say. They may appreciate being tape-recorded if they know that only the interviewer will listen to it. They understand if the interviewer takes notes. Try to capture the most salient points as verbatim quotes. You will want to review your notes or the tape as soon after the interview as possible, while your memory is fresh. When you have completed your interviews, go back and look for anomalies as well as patterns in the responses. Use what you learn in one interview to help you prepare for the next one. As you learn more from people, you may find yourself developing new questions or changing your perspective. Each interview offers you the opportunity to deepen your understanding.

Focus Groups

Focus groups are really just group interviews. They are a good way to bring together small groups of people with similar characteristics to talk about—and focus on—a particular issue or topic. You might want to talk with a representative sample of the people who might benefit from or use a possible new service or program. If you have uncovered enough data to suggest that a homework center for teens might be a desirable new service, you might want to talk to teens to find out what kinds of homework help they really need. Do they need a quiet place to study? Or a space for working on group projects?

Would homework helpers or tutors be useful? What about computers and specialized databases? Be sure to talk to a range of students from straight-A college-bound types to those who are struggling to get by. You might discover that the teens need or want a performance venue or a makerspace, where they can create three-dimensional items to help them apply learning, more than a homework center. It's better to learn this before you invest in an unwanted new service.

There isn't a magic number for participants in a focus group, either. You want enough people that a variety of opinions are represented, but not so many that people will feel uncomfortable speaking up. Somewhere between 7 and 10 usually works well. They can sit around a table and make eye contact with the facilitator and with each other. We have learned that people are more likely to feel comfortable in a focus group setting if they have something to do with their hands. We like to provide paper and marking pens, Play-Doh, or pipe cleaners. Easy-to-eat snacks are always a good idea, too. Follow the guidelines for posing questions and recording responses that we presented in the section above on interviews.

How many focus groups do you need to hold? If the community is divided on an issue at the heart of your proposed new service, you will want to be sure you hear all sides. If there are multiple stakeholders, you will want to hear from all of them. Generally, professional researchers recommend that you continue to hold focus groups until you can predict the major responses. This usually happens after three or four sessions. You will need to decide what kind of trade-offs to make in the interest of rigor and effort expended.

Surveys

Surveys tend to be more useful during the evaluation phase of OBPE, but there are some ways they can add to your data as you assess the community. Surveys have the advantage of reaching potentially more people than you can target with either interviews or focus groups. If you have access to a group of significant stakeholders or potential users of a possible new service or program, administering a well-designed survey could yield very relevant information. For example, a survey of Head Start parents or WIC recipients could tell you whether your idea for a family literacy program appeals to them. You could try out your idea for a play-reading or book discussion program with regulars at the local senior citizens center.

Constructing a good survey is not as easy as it looks. Think carefully about what you want to learn and construct one question for each aspect of the issue or piece of information you need. Frame the question in clear, unambiguous terms, avoiding jargon and technical terms, and state the question in positive terms. Of course, you should always be aware of situations in which translations into other languages may be necessary. We have found that short surveys, limited to one page, are the most effective for most purposes. Also, think about how you want to structure participants' responses. Should they be open-ended? Fixed, multiple choice responses? Yes/no or agree/disagree? Rating on a Likert scale? Don't forget that you will have to eventually code the responses.

Do plan to test your questionnaire with a small pilot group. You will save yourself a lot of trouble by learning that the question you thought was so clear is actually confusing to your intended respondents. You may also discover that you have failed to ask about something that is actually central to your future plans. This gives you an opportunity to rethink your survey before committing it to your target group. In order to analyze the data, you will need to collate the responses to each question and apply some kind of statistical calculation. It may be enough to just calculate totals and apply percentages; you almost certainly don't need to worry about advanced techniques, such as standard deviation.

ANALYZING THE RESULTS

You have been conducting qualitative research, which aims at generating an in-depth understanding of some aspect of human behavior in a particular case or setting. You are aiming to understand the behavior and opinions of a particular set of people in the community your library serves in order to better provide resources that meet their needs. If you have chosen to conduct a thorough community assessment, you have now amassed a considerable amount of data: community contact information, lists of relevant local resources, demographics and other statistics, opinions and feedback from stakeholders, community residents, and various key informants. How can you make sense of all of this material?

First, get your bits and pieces of data organized. Pull it together in one place. If it's stored on a computer, print it so you and your assessment team can share and take it apart again, if necessary. Now is the time to revisit your "Research Methods 101" coursework for a review of some basic analytical techniques. The first research term to understand is *triangulation*. As a research method, triangulation is simply the application of more than one methodological approach to study a particular phenomenon. It has the advantage of bringing several perspectives to bear on the subject being studied and is often used as a way to bring credibility to qualitative analysis. If you have used published statistical documents, interviews, and observations in the conduct of your community assessment, you are now able to bring the data together to arrive at a credible account.

The simplest way to arrive at that account is to look for patterns that emerge from your various data sources. For example, you may have learned from published statistics that the high school gradu-ation rate in your community is lower than the state average. You have also discovered, through your own observations and from key informants—the teens and counselors from the high school—that there are no free or low-cost tutoring services available. The director of a recreation center that draws a lot of teens to its facility has told you that they would like to offer homework help, but don't have the resources to do so. Taken together, these separate items of informa-tion point to a pattern that includes both a community need—aca-demic support for high school students—and an asset—the possible partnership opportunity with the recreation center.

Another analytical tool you can use is "recursive abstraction" or "successive reduction of data." These unwieldy technical terms refer to a means of compacting data in order to detect patterns that might not be otherwise apparent. In its simplest form, this technique involves summarizing data from a particular source—perhaps your focus group notes—and highlighting the most important findings. You then take the highlighted statements and summarize them, until you see patterns or themes emerging. Do these patterns or themes line up with abstracted data from other sources, such as interviews or statistics?

The manual and worksheets, developed by the Harwood Institute for Public Innovation (2014) for the American Library Association, include some excellent models and templates for summarizing what you have learned through your community assessment efforts. One is the creation of a "Community Narrative Template":

> Families want (*aspirations*), but they're concerned about (*main concerns*). People talk specifically about (*specific issues*). They believe we need to focus on (*actions*). If (*particular groups or individuals*) played a part in those actions, folks would be more likely to trust the effort and step forward.

The template articulates a particular community aspiration and points the way to possible service responses. There is an example of a hypothetical community narrative in chapter 5.

By now you should have established a few salient findings from the work you did as you hunted for relevant community data. You may have begun this quest with only a general desire to learn more about the everyday lives, interests, and concerns of a particular part of your community's population: teens, parents of preschool children, senior citizens, or Spanish-speaking families. Or you may have wanted to learn whether a potential service or program would be appropriate for your community. Hopefully, you are now ready to develop outcomes based on your community assessment and to plan the service or program that will deliver those desired outcomes. The next chapter tells you how to derive outcomes from your community assessment, as outlined in Phase II of the OBPE flow chart.

REFERENCES

Hacker, Karen. 2013. *Community-Based Participatory Research*. Los Angeles: Sage.

Harwood Institute for Public Innovation. 2014. "Libraries Transforming Communities: LTC Public Innovators Cohort." www.ala.org/transforminglibraries/libraries-transforming -communities/cohort.

"Santa Monica Public Library Mission and Vision." smpl.org/ Mission_and_Vision.aspx.

"Santa Monica Public Library Policies." smpl.org/policies.aspx.

Stringer, Ernest T. 2014. *Action Research*. 4th ed. Los Angeles: Sage.

3

Determining Outcomes

NOW THAT YOU HAVE IDENTIFIED YOUR COMMUNITY'S interests, needs, aspirations, and concerns, you can begin thinking about how the library might better serve the public through targeted and intentional programs and services. But first, you must determine how the community will benefit from the library's new or enhanced services or programs. These anticipated benefits are the outcomes, which are designated in Phase II of the outcome-based planning and evaluation process.

DEFINING TERMS

Outcomes can be a difficult concept to grasp, so let's review some of the terms we have already discussed. Although some may call them "goals," outcomes specifically identify the positive change that occurs as a result of using the library. Such change may result from gaining a new or enhanced *skill,* acquiring new *knowledge,* taking on a different or improved *attitude,* modifying one's *behavior,* or improving one's life *status* or *condition.* Typical library outcomes include learning how to use an e-book reader through one-on-one customer training (new skill); becoming more informed about current events thanks to a monthly book discussion group (new knowledge); gaining confidence by participating in the library's literacy program (improved attitude); starting a walking club as a result of attending a healthy-living program at the library (modified behavior); and getting a job after using the library's career center (improved status/condition). These are just some of the life situations you can positively impact by launching an OBPE project. Outcomes may be considered goals, but because they end in a particular result, not all goals are outcomes. As you will soon see, unlike goals, which tend to express broad expectations, outcomes are very specific in their intent.

Outcomes are also different from two other similar terms: *inputs* and *outputs.* Although they came into vogue in the 1980s and '90s, when the American Library Association published a series of books on how to collect "output measures," reporting inputs and outputs remains relevant today and is still important when designing and evaluating the library's services and programs. Inputs and outputs are related to outcomes; but they, by themselves, do not reflect the difference the library makes in the lives of its users. So how do inputs and outputs differ from outcomes and each other?

Inputs

Inputs are the internal resources the library uses to provide a service or program. These include staff, the collection, computers, meeting rooms, furniture, vehicles to deliver materials, supplies, and whatever else is needed to implement the library's mission. Identifying the availability of these resources is absolutely critical when planning any new service or program. This is why we encourage you to complete an internal environmental scan (appendix A) before planning any new project. The library's career center, for instance, will have little impact if not adequately staffed or well stocked with relevant materials. Indeed, outcomes cannot be accomplished without inputs. Nevertheless, no matter how many books, computers, or chairs a library owns, they have little value unless they are used to effect positive change in the community.

Outputs

Outputs measure the usage of the library's resources and are expressed as quantities. Typical outputs include circulation and in-library use of materials; the number of people who visit the library, either in person or virtually; reference tallies; program attendance; and library card registrations. Usually reported as annual statistics, outputs are important because they record the volume of work the library has accomplished. Statistical up-and-down usage patterns are often analyzed to determine how well the library is serving its community. If door-count and circulation remain stable or increase, then you and your governing body may consider this a sign of good service. But what do these numbers really mean? Outputs merely report *how much* service the library provides.

Outcomes, on the other hand, demonstrate the *value* of that service. It's one thing to report that thirty learners participated in the library's literacy program during the month of May. It's quite another to report that, as a result of participating in the literacy program, one learner was finally able to take his driver's license exam and another can now read to her children. Outputs count the number of people who participate in a library program—for example, thirty literacy learners—while outcomes tell *why* the program was created in the first place—that is, to improve people's lives. Both data are important; but it is outcomes (results) that put usage statistics (outputs) into true perspective.

CREATING OUTCOME STATEMENTS

Once the community assessment is complete, the OBPE team, made up of library staff and relevant stakeholders (as described in chapter

2), reviews the data collected and begins to look for evidence of the target population's top priorities. Let's say, for example, that interviews with teachers and several parents of middle school-aged children reveal that many students are failing math. This, then, might become the focus of a library program aimed at serving middle school students and their families. The community expresses a troubling need, which the library decides to help address. The next step is to determine the outcome the library hopes to effect.

There are many ways to help students who are failing math. You might decide to make math textbooks available in the library or you may be prompted to offer a formal after-school math assistance program or online tutoring. A strong public service ethic frequently motivates librarians to respond quickly to their surroundings, often without giving much thought to ultimate results. Ill-planned, knee-jerk reactions to addressing the community's needs usually take a "band-aid" approach to problem solving and so may, in fact, do little good because the consequences were never considered. To avoid this pitfall, you must first determine what the library hopes to accomplish by addressing the community's concerns. Only after determining a desired outcome can you devise a strategy to achieve that outcome. This type of results-based planning is sometimes called "backward design" and can be rather disorienting to problem-solvers, like librarians, who tend to think in a linear fashion. Nonetheless, by identifying the ultimate outcome first, you are forced to constantly keep the end result in mind when planning library programs and services.

After gathering all the data required to fully understand the concerns about youngsters failing math, you decide to create a library program that will achieve the following outcome:

> "Remedial middle school students comprehend math
>   homework."

If accomplished, this outcome will result in the students gaining *knowledge,* one of the six areas of benefit that libraries should target when determining outcomes. You will notice that the outcome is written in the present tense, even though it indicates something that will eventually be accomplished. Because it represents an end result, it is written as a declaration—"Remedial middle school students comprehend math homework" (present tense)—rather than as a goal—"Remedial middle school students *will* comprehend math homework" (future tense). The outcome statement is also very simple. There is a subject ("remedial middle school students"), a verb ("comprehend"), and an object ("math homework"): the simpler the statement, the better, so everyone understands what you're trying to achieve. The most important thing is that, as a result of participating in the library's program, kids who previously failed math now comprehend their homework.

Outcome statements are community focused and so should always reflect benefits to the users, not to the library. Librarians tend to think the lives of all people would improve a hundred-fold if only they used the library more often. While we may share this sentiment, we want to challenge you to create outcome statements that do not just describe a change in your target population's library habits. Rather, the outcome should reflect the positive change in a person's life *as a result of using the library*. This is a subtle but important difference in how outcome statements should be written. For instance, one result of creating a math homework program might be that young people, who never used the library before, now visit at least one afternoon a week. We know this is a terrific by-product of the program. But, in the context of responding to the community's identified need, what do these visits ultimately achieve? Coming to the library to do homework is just a means of accomplishing the overall end, which, in this case, is to help remedial middle school students better understand math. Increasing the number of students who visit the library after school is an output. Helping those students succeed academically is the desired outcome.

For this reason, too, the outcome statement is focused on a very specific target population. You may want to help all middle school students comprehend their math homework. Realistically, however, this would be nearly impossible for one library to do. You therefore decide to focus your efforts on helping a small, identifiable group of children who, it appears, need more assistance than others. Being "remedial" already indicates a need for improvement. Outcomes aim to change people's lives in a positive way. Targeting a specific group of students, who you know will benefit from your service, helps you designate an achievable and measurable outcome.

INDICATORS OF OUTCOME ACHIEVEMENT

Whatever outcomes you hope to effect, you must be able to measure whether or not you accomplished what you set out to achieve. Are the middle school students indeed getting the help they need to comprehend their math homework? Progress toward accomplishing an outcome is measured through benchmarks, called "indicators," which, as their name suggests, indicate whether or not your end result is achieved. Indicators specify certain benchmarks that lead to accomplishing the stated outcome. As a personal example, let's say you decide to set an outcome of improving your health, resulting in a positive change in your condition. Some indicators of improved health might be exhibited in lowering your blood pressure by 20 points, losing 10 pounds, or being able to walk 2 miles in 30 minutes. Achievement of any or all of these targeted factors provides evidence of improved health and helps determine whether or not you actually reached your ultimate outcome. Measuring improved health can be a difficult concept to wrap your head around, but with specific indicators that are observable (e.g., weight loss and lowered blood pressure), you measure whether or not you achieved your outcome. Indicators, therefore, define what success looks like.

Every outcome should have at least one indicator that determines achievement. When identifying indicators, you should ask yourself, "How will we know we have achieved what we set out to accomplish?" Our hypothetical outcome promises that remedial middle school students will get the help needed to understand their math homework. Possible indicators of success include an increased rate of homework completion; testimonies from math tutors, parents, and the kids themselves that they better understand their school assignments; and a higher rate of passing math class. In all cases, the desired outcome and its indicators determine what we hope to accomplish and so inform what type of service or program we offer to help middle-schoolers comprehend their math homework. Indicators also measure achievement and so are a big part of evaluation (OBPE Phase IV) as discussed in chapter 5.

USING STANDARDIZED OUTCOME STATEMENTS

Sometimes it is more efficient to use outcome statements, developed and tested by others, than it is to create your own, especially if you have never used outcomes to plan and evaluate services before. Using someone else's statements might also allow you to compare your services to libraries that are working toward the same outcomes. The five-step OBPE process would still be the same; but instead of creating original outcomes, you would adopt statements successfully tested by others. Several years ago, Virginia Walter and Cindy Mediavilla received an ALA research grant to test six positive youth development outcomes specified in the Urban Libraries Council's Public Libraries as Partners in Youth Development Project. The six outcomes, which we used to measure the effectiveness of teen-based homework help programs, were:

1. Youth contribute to their community.
2. They feel safe in their environment.
3. They have meaningful relationships with adults and peers.
4. They achieve educational success.
5. They develop marketable skills.
6. They develop personal and social skills.

We found that not only were these outcomes indeed achievable in teen-based homework help programs, but any of them would provide an effective framework for designing and evaluating such programs (Walter and Mediavilla 2003; Walter and Meyers 2003, 93–97).

In California, the State Library and the California Library Association have partnered to offer the Summer Reading Challenge, a statewide initiative that encourages public libraries to use outcomes to plan and evaluate their summer reading programs. To motivate librarians to adopt OBPE in carrying out their summer programs, the following two outcome statements were developed and tested for use at the local level:

1. Children/teens/adults/families belong to a community of readers and library users
2. Underserved community members participate in the summer reading program

The first outcome builds on research showing that summer reading participants tend to be active and engaged readers who use libraries. Therefore, the emphasis is on children, teens, adults, and families who already benefit from using the library. The second outcome, however, focuses on community outreach and encourages libraries to find ways to attract non-library users. Both statements are widely relevant, yet specific enough, to generate meaningful data. When several libraries target the same summer reading outcomes, results can be more easily compared and trends more readily identified. In fact, the ALA includes the California Summer Reading Challenge on its list of summer reading "best practices" (California Library Association n.d.; Cole, Walter, and Mitnick 2013).

The Public Library Association recently released Project Outcome, a national initiative that provides a standardized process for measuring the impact of public library services. The field-tested project makes available a template for creating outcome statements and offers standardized survey instruments for measuring library programs in seven areas: civic/community engagement; digital inclusion (i.e., services to access technology, build technology-related skills and confidence, and make beneficial use of digital content); early childhood literacy; economic development (e.g., small business training and personal finance management); education/lifelong learning; job skills; and summer reading. The hope is that, by using standard outcome measurements, public librarians around the country will be able to aggregate the results of their service and speak with one voice when advocating on behalf of their libraries (Davis and Plagman 2015; Teasdale 2015).

Whether you create your own statement or borrow one from others, the next step is to design a program or service that will help accomplish your outcome. This is Phase III in the OBPE process and is discussed further in chapter 4.

REFERENCES

California Library Association. "California Summer Reading Challenge: Outcomes-Based Summer Reading." calchallenge .org/evaluation/outcomes/.

Cole, Natalie, Virginia Walter, and Eva Mitnick. 2013. "Outcomes + Outreach: The California Summer Reading Outcomes Initiative." *Public Libraries* 52 (March/April). publiclibrariesonline.org/ 2013/05/outcomes/.

Davis, Denise, and Emily Plagman. 2015. "Project Outcome: Helping Libraries Capture Their Community Impact." *Public Libraries* 54 (July/August): 33–37.

Teasdale, Rebecca. 2015. "Project Outcome Launch—Seven Surveys to Measure Impact." *Public Libraries Online* (May 28). publiclibrariesonline.org/2015/05/project-outcome-launch -seven-surveys-to-measure-impact/.

Walter, Virginia, and Cindy Mediavilla. 2003. "Homework Center Outcomes." UCLA Department of Information Studies. is-intranet.gseis.ucla.edu/research/homework/.

Walter, Virginia A., and Elaine Meyers. 2003. *Teens & Libraries: Getting It Right.* Chicago: American Library Association.

4

Designing Programs and Services

W E HAVE NOW REACHED THE THIRD STEP OF THE FIVE-
step outcome-based planning and evaluation process. Like
each of the two steps or phases before this, it follows naturally from
the phase before it. The program or service you plan and implement
should be designed to meet the outcome or outcomes you identified
in Phase II. Those outcomes, in turn, should have been a response to
needs identified in Phase I. These programs or services you design in
Phase III should help the library's community fulfill its unmet aspirations in some way. Here, too, is where your own professional education and experience come together with the "street knowledge" you
have gathered to create added value. You will be putting the library's
resources to work on behalf of the community.

MIDDLE SCHOOL STUDENTS AND MATH: A CASE STUDY

It would be a mistake to turn inward at this point in the planning process, abandoning all of the contacts and potential partners you identified during your community assessment. Take the outcome presented as an example in chapter 3: "Remedial middle school students comprehend math homework." Presumably you derived this outcome after analyzing data from a number of sources: focus groups or interviews with parents and teachers, standardized test scores, and conversations with the students themselves. If you and your community assessment team had created a "Community Narrative Template," it might have looked something like this:

> People want middle school students to do well in school, but they are concerned that they lack the skills to pass their math class and do well on the standardized math tests. Students who have fallen behind say they don't understand their math assignments. As people talk more about those concerns, they talk specifically about poor preparation in elementary school and parents' inability to help their children with their homework. They believe we need to focus on remedial help for the students, after-school homework help, and workshops to help parents understand the way middle school math is taught. They also believe that, if the local schools played a part in those actions, folks would be more likely to trust the effort and step forward.

A first step might be to reconvene the assessment team and confirm that a narrative like this accurately reflects the community's ideas and opinions. Ask for their ideas on ways the community's concerns might be addressed. Don't be surprised if members of the community have very traditional ideas about what role the library could play. At this point you could share with them some of the library staff's ideas about the kinds of programs and services that might be feasible.

Staff may consider developing a full-service homework center, similar to the model described in *Creating the Full-Service Homework*

Center in Your Library (Mediavilla 2001). Upon considering the available resources, you and your team decide that this is a more complex commitment and so decide to begin seeking long-term funding for such an endeavor. However, you also want to demonstrate to community members that you heard their issues and are ready to act. You decide that, beginning with the next academic year, you will offer after-school math tutoring one day a week during the academic year. You will work with the teen librarian and middle school math teachers to identify students who are falling behind and send them special invitations to participate in the program. The teen librarian will supervise and train a small group of high school and college education major volunteers to help the younger students.

The tutoring program, meeting in the community room and staffed with friendly, approachable people who are competent to help young teens with their math homework, will be the ongoing part of your service response to this outcome. However, you may also want to address the other concerns that were raised: poor preparation in elementary school and parents' lack of confidence in their ability to help their children. You might want to assemble an ad hoc advisory group to help you design appropriate responses to these issues. This would be a good time to approach community partners to see what kind of support they could offer. (We will address the issue of collaborations and partnerships a little later in this chapter.) There is a lot of interest currently in science, technology, engineering, and math (STEM) programs for young people. If you frame your idea as a STEM project, it may attract some funding. You may want to dress it up a little to make it more attractive to the students as well as funders. Call it a club or a boot camp and link it with the other elements of STEM. You can even add art, as some libraries are doing, and develop a STEAM program with heavy doses of math as the basis for art (Koester 2014). Makerspaces are a great way to get young people involved in real-life applications of math and science principles (Klipper 2014; Pisarski 2014).

Finally, you will want to address the needs of the parents whose math background is limited or out-of-date. Again a partnership with the middle school and perhaps the education department of a local college would be advisable. Go back to your advisory group and talk about specifics like time, place, and format. Do the parents speak English, or would it be better if the instruction were given in another language? Would they be comfortable coming to the library for a workshop, or would they rather go to the school? Or another venue entirely, like a local church or business? Are both fathers and mothers likely to come? Would you need to offer babysitting services? Would it be appropriate to design a workshop for both students and their parents? This might be an effective way to engage both parties in collaborative learning.

You decide that for your first year you will try offering one-time workshops in both Spanish and English that are intended to help parents understand how their students are being taught math. The middle school math teacher, who is also part of your OBPE team, agrees to teach the two workshops. You will offer the workshops on Saturday mornings at the library and provide coffee and pastries as an enticement for participation. You must also think about a budget for your new initiative. Will the outlay be modest enough to manage with existing resources? Will your Friends group or foundation be able to support the venture? If you need to apply for grant funding, you will be in a strong competitive position because of the investment you made earlier in doing a good needs assessment and your ongoing engagement with community partners.

Your advisory group and staff will probably bring up other details to think about. You may want to come up with a name that encompasses the three basic elements of this initiative: Math Magic, Math at the Library, or Math for Everybody. (We know you can do better than this; this is just to give you an idea.) Develop a timetable, especially if you are implementing the initiative in stages. Don't forget the need for publicity.

It is also important to start looking ahead to the last phase of the OBPE process: evaluation. You will almost certainly want to be making some baseline "before" assessments. You probably can't get data about individual students' math grades, but you should be able to get aggregate data about math grades or math scores related to the local school. If students are required to register for the tutoring program, then they can take a pre-test as part of the registration process. A post-test would then be administered at the end of either the first semester or the school year.

If you continue to have meaningful formal and informal conversations with the people who live in your community and who use—or could potentially use—your library services, you increase the likelihood that those services will continue to be both excellent and relevant. You will know immediately, for example, if students feel uncomfortable seeing their teachers at the library after school. You will get instant feedback on the activities and lessons being conducted in the tutoring program. You will know whether or not the parents are getting what they need from the workshops offered for them. These kinds of informal evaluations help you make small adjustments as you go along so you won't be taken by surprise when you do a more formal summative evaluation at the end.

OTHER SCENARIOS

The previous example of an outcome that led to an initiative to help middle school students do better in math is only one scenario, of course. The service initiative described above is a fairly intensive response to an issue raised by members of the community. However, it is a response that fits expectations of typical library services. Other outcomes may require more or less effort to meet expectations by designing relevant library services and programs, or they may call for services that fall outside the library's usual areas of expertise.

In the OBPE workshops we conducted in California, during the summer of 2015, some participants voiced their concerns after developing outcomes for a hypothetical community case study. They protested that they're not psychologists or social workers or any number of specialized professionals that might be needed to fully realize a community's aspirations. This is when the library needs to look back to its initial community assessment and identify potential partners. For example, another outcome that has been voiced in some community assessments is: "Small business operators acquire useful information about marketing." In addressing this concern, the library might enlist help from the local merchants' association and the local office of the Small Business Administration (SBA). The service response could be as simple and basic as developing and publicizing a special collection of books and databases to meet the need. A series of workshops on low-cost marketing strategies led by SBA staff or local college instructors would be an additional way to add value to the collection and give the participants an opportunity to voice their concerns. As the small business operators, SBA staff, local politicians, and librarians continue to meet and develop mutual trust and respect, they might decide to collaborate on an annual street fair to highlight their unique offerings. Each of these programs escalates the investment of resources and potential payoff in positive outcomes.

In another hypothetical scenario, perhaps your community assessment revealed concerns about the lack of healthy produce available to local residents. Possible partners might be concerned individuals, public health workers, and representatives from agencies of the Department of Agriculture as well as elected officials. These advisors might work with library staff to identify a location for a community garden and an appropriate agency to supervise it. Library staff could develop a special collection of gardening books, offer workshops on urban gardening, and perhaps even create a seed library (Weak 2014).

A WORD ABOUT PARTNERSHIPS

Collaboration has become a preferred strategy for entrepreneurial public enterprise. The idea is that two organizations or agencies can do more together than either can do alone. Many funding agencies, including the Institute of Museum and Library Services, give preference to proposals that foster strong and relevant partnerships. OBPE, with its focus on community assessment, tends to lead naturally to the identification of potential partners for collaborative ventures. The best of these partnerships are more than opportunistic or accidental unions; they are intentional initiatives that create value and enhance existing services.

After doing an extensive assessment of their patrons' use patterns and unmet needs, the staff at the Deschutes Public Library in central Oregon discovered that many people in the community were unaware of the library's resources. Responding at first to what they perceived to be the library's lack of visibility, administration sent staff out into the community to meet people, particularly those involved with civic organizations. These "community librarians" developed new relationships that evolved into twenty formal partnerships and many informal ones. Deborah Fallows (2015), who wrote an article for *The Atlantic* about the Deschutes Public Library, closes with this formula for library success: "Know your users; partner with the community; identify the needs; offer solutions to problems (even before they become problems); and act with enthusiasm."

Apparently, staff at the Deschutes Public Library got it right. But problems can arise as you work with community partners to develop and implement your new programs and services. Being aware of the following typical roadblocks can help you avoid them or at least weaken their impact:

- People charged with implementing the venture may be less committed to the project than the top-level decision-makers who initiated it.

- Lower-level staff may fail to see the larger positive implications of the venture and see only its problems.

- Most of the staff involved with the project have other primary responsibilities to which they are more committed.

- Some staff may actually try to sabotage the new venture because it represents a threat to their own interests.

- Differences in culture and operating procedures may make it difficult for staff from the two organizations to work together.

- People may, through ignorance or laziness, resort to stereotyping individuals and groups in the partner organization, creating a cycle of mistrust that is difficult to break.

Here are some tested strategies for making partnerships work:

- Be prepared to make an investment in time and resources.
- Invite the right people to the table from the beginning: include those who will be implementing the partnership activities as well as the key decision-makers.
- Design communication channels that build respect and trust among the participants.
- Ensure that the key participants connect personally with the collaboration's purpose and with each other.
- Look for partnership opportunities in which there is congruence of mission, strategy, and values among the collaborators.
- Seek partnership opportunities that create value, enabling the collaborators to accomplish something positive that neither could do alone.

One final piece of advice: Don't take on too many partnerships. One strategic partner may be enough. Once you become a visible player in the life of your community, you may get more requests to collaborate than you can reasonably handle.

Each desired outcome presents different challenges in implementing services. You will need to set priorities as you decide which of the many community needs and concerns are most appropriate for the library to tackle. Most libraries will use the detailed five-step OBPE process, outlined in this book, for no more than one or two major service initiatives. The following section provides a guide for moving ahead with the design of a new service, like the ones described above, after getting approval from the required authority in your library.

DESIGNING LIBRARY SERVICES
TO BENEFIT THE COMMUNITY

Effective public librarians understand that engaging community members in ongoing conversations is as important to the success of their mission as collection development, reference and readers' advisory services, or early childhood literacy programs. We were interested in reading about the Working Together Project in Canada that sent community development librarians into diverse neighborhoods in Vancouver, Regina, Toronto, and Halifax. They worked with populations that were traditionally considered socially isolated or excluded—for example, immigrants and refugees, people living in poverty, youth at risk, people recently released from penal institutions, or those of aboriginal descent. Over the four years of the project, community-based librarians engaged directly with people in these groups to develop services driven by their lived experiences, rather than by the librarians' professional understanding. They also developed authentic relationships, based on trust and mutual respect with community members. As a result, a new model of community-led service planning emerged. Unlike traditional service planning models, the Working Together approach depends on the relationships between library staff and community members. Service ideas come from the community; staff members act as partners and facilitators, rather than as creators. Community partners work with the staff to deliver the services (Williment 2011). The project, which was financially supported through agreements with Human Resources and Social Development Canada, may sound impractical without special funding. However, the underlying idea is worth a wider discussion in the public library community, as we work to adapt our traditional services to evolving expectations from our users, our policy-makers, and the broader community.

In another example, the Hartford Public Library in Connecticut was one of the pilot projects in the ALA's Libraries Transforming Communities initiative, a partnership with the Harwood Institute for Public Innovation. As a result of their community assessment process, staff learned that the community's main concerns were public safety, community violence, and their relationship with the police. The library responded with a series of community dialogues between the residents and the police that helped to build trust where there had been suspicion and distrust (Marcotte 2015).

Book-to-Action is an initiative that began at the Multnomah County Library and is now being funded with modest small grants by the California State Library. The program starts out much like a traditional book discussion group, in that participants, mostly adults, get together to read and talk about a book that has been chosen for its relevance to community engagement. The project's toolkit suggests titles that support thirteen different themes, such as "Immigrants and Refugees," "Rescuing an Animal," "Homelessness, Poverty, Hunger, and Hard Times," and "Women's Rights and Empowerment of Girls" (California State Library n.d.). The library then invites the author or a subject expert to speak to the readers, who select a civic engagement project to build on the themes of the book they read together. A community partner is involved from the beginning. Among the projects, implemented in 2014, was a "knit-in" to make hats and scarves for young cancer patients in Nevada County (after reading John Green's *The Fault in Our Stars*), and a series of events in Oakland to promote biking after reading *Everyday Bicycling* by Elly Blue (California State Library 2014).

What is different about the Canadian project and initiatives, like Book-to-Action and the Turning Outward approach outlined by the Harwood Institute, is that they are not focused on improving the library or even the individual library user. Rather, they are focused on using the library's resources to improve the community. Obviously, responsible librarians will continue to strive to make their facilities and services as excellent as possible, by recruiting the best possible staff and continuing to hone traditional library skills. They will also lead the way in developing expertise in new technologies and media. But by developing skills in planning and evaluation and community outreach, they will add value to those traditional skills and do a great deal to enhance the library's role in its community.

REFERENCES

California State Library. "Book-to-Action Libraries." 2014. www.library.ca.gov/lds/getinvolved/booktoaction//lib_list2014 .html.

California State Library. "Book-to-Action Toolkit." www.library. ca.gov/lds/getinvolved/booktoaction/.

Fallows, Deborah. 2015. "A Library of Good Ideas." *The Atlantic,* August 2. www.theatlantic.com/national/archive/2015/08/ a-library-of-good-ideas/400259/.

Klipper, Barbara. 2014. "Making Makerspaces Work for Everyone: Lessons in Accessibility." *Children and Libraries* 12 (Fall): 5–6.

Koester, Amy. 2014. "Get STEAM Rolling! Demystifying STEAM and Finding the Right Fit for Your Library." *Children and Libraries* 12 (Fall): 22–25.

Marcotte, Alison. 2015. "Hartford Public Library Builds, Strengthens Community-Police Relations." *American Libraries,* August 3. americanlibrariesmagazine.org/authors/alison -marcotte/.

Mediavilla, Cindy. 2001. *Creating the Full-Service Homework Center in Your Library.* Chicago: American Library Association.

Pisarski, Alyssa. 2014. "Finding a Place for the Tween: Makerspaces and Libraries." *Children and Libraries* 12 (Fall): 13–16.

Weak, Emily. 2014. "Simple Steps to Starting a Seed Library." *Public Libraries* 53 (July/August): 24–26.

Williment, Kenneth. 2011. "It Takes a Community to Create a Library." *Public Libraries* 50 (March/April): 30–35.

5

Evaluating Programs and Services

IN MANY LIBRARIES, PROGRAM EVALUATION OCCURS almost as an afterthought. Staff may plan and deliver a program and then, perhaps at the last minute, pull together a survey to ask participants their opinion about what they had just experienced. Or data may be collected at the end of a grant project or as part of the library's annual report. In these cases, evaluation is often grudgingly treated as a bothersome, yet required, exercise that staff must undertake. Nevertheless, a well-planned evaluation can be a critical means of validating the good work the library does. After all, without evaluation, how will we know we have achieved what we set out to do? If library programs are the mechanism by which outcomes are achieved, evaluation is the means by which the effectiveness of those programs is measured. Therefore, even though it's listed as Phase IV of the OBPE process, an evaluation strategy should be developed at the same time you plan your programs and services.

INDICATORS OF SUCCESS

Although staff tend to be brilliant at planning library programs, many are less brilliant at measuring the impact of those programs, possibly because little thought has gone into creating an evaluation strategy. Much like outcome statements, which are developed before programs and services are implemented, an evaluation plan should be designed well before any actual evaluation occurs. In fact, evaluation should be considered at the same time you develop the programs and services that will help achieve the stated outcome. As you design each new program, you should ask yourselves, "How will we know this program is a success?" This, then, naturally leads to the designation of targeted benchmarks that will help measure whether or not the program is successful. These targets are the indicators that define what success looks like.

In chapter 3, we addressed community concerns about youngsters' lack of math proficiency by creating a hypothetical outcome promising that remedial middle school students will comprehend math homework. We then suggested, in chapter 4, potential strategies for achieving this outcome, including offering weekly after-school math tutoring in the library. We also recommended conducting math workshops for parents; but after careful consideration and more research into staff capacity, you decided the library wasn't quite ready to offer two programs. For one thing, the parents of many of the remedial students speak only Spanish and you haven't been able to find a math instructor who is fluent in Spanish. If the tutoring program is successful this year, you will consider expanding it to include parents next year.

Once you decide which service strategies to pursue, you then designate realistic benchmarks to help you measure achievement of the outcome and its programs. Comprehension of math homework, for instance, can be measured in many ways. Certainly a successful math-tutoring program will lead to a higher percentage of homework completion. Parents may also report that their children have an improved attitude toward math and the tutors may notice a marked improvement in students' math skills. Moreover, the kids themselves may say they now understand their homework better as a result of being tutored at the library. In fact, the program may be so effective that a majority of participants, who failed last year, will pass math this year. Any or all of these measurements can provide evidence of outcome achievement and so are indicators of the program's success.

Because they help ascertain whether or not the outcome has been achieved, indicators should be expressed in clearly measurable terms. This means they should set numerical goals and state a deadline by which the benchmark will be measured. Although, as librarians, we want all of our users to benefit from our services 100 percent of the time, in reality this just isn't practical. For one thing, not everything is within our control nor do all community members share our goals. Therefore, you need to be reasonable in indicating expectations. We recommend setting a well-informed but modest target, especially at first—perhaps a 50 percent success rate or even lower. If you exceed this target, you can congratulate yourself on a job well done and raise the bar next time around. But if you don't meet the target, then you use your findings to assess why and make adjustments. The point is to designate indicators that are challenging enough to make the effort worthwhile, but not too lofty to accomplish.

In our hypothetical case study, we anticipate that remedial middle school students will better comprehend their math homework as a result of weekly tutoring at the library. As mentioned above, achievement of this outcome can be measured in several ways. The simplest indication of success might be an increased number of completed math assignments. Since the students will be working intensely with tutors, it is not unreasonable to expect that at least 60 percent of program participants will complete their homework, on a weekly basis, by the end of the first semester. While this percentage may seem impossibly high at the start of the school year, the target should be achievable by midyear if the tutors and students work together to accomplish it. Your first indicator then is as follows:

> At least 60 percent of program participants will complete their homework, on a weekly basis, by the end of the first semester.

The indicator is quantitative—you have targeted homework completion by 60 percent of students participating in the program—and gives a deadline (i.e., the end of the first semester) by which this particular outcome element will be accomplished. So far, this seems rather straightforward and relatively easy to measure. Let's now look at other possible outcome indicators.

The tutors and the students themselves will no doubt have opinions on how well the program is progressing. Therefore, two other indicators might be:

> By the end of the first semester, 50 percent of participants will say they understand their math homework better.

> By the end of the first semester, tutors will report improvement in 45 percent of the participants' math skills.

Although these benchmarks may seem low—after all, we'd prefer to see 100 percent improvement—they are nonetheless realistic and help you measure the progress of your projected outcome. Because these indicators occur midyear, you may also want to set targets for the end of the year and so designate the following:

> By the end of the school year, 65 percent of parents will report that their child has an improved attitude toward math.

> At the end of the school year, 85 percent of program participants will pass math.

Again, we may hope that the program is 100 percent successful, but uncontrollable factors will inevitably intervene to preclude this from happening. Expecting that 65 percent of the students will develop a more positive attitude toward math seems realistic, as does a passing rate of 85 percent. Both indicators are measurable, have deadlines (i.e., the end of the school year), and provide evidence of outcome achievement. As illustrated in figure 5.1, the outcome informs your service plan, which is then measured by the indicators. We will now discuss how to create a strategy for evaluating whether or not your indicators have been met.

FIGURE 5.1

Case Study Example

COMMUNITY ASSESSMENT FINDINGS	OUTCOME STATEMENT	OUTCOME-BASED LIBRARY PROGRAM	OUTCOME INDICATORS
Parents and teachers are concerned that middle school students are failing math	Remedial middle school students comprehend math homework	After-school math tutoring program, offered weekly in the library	At least 60% of program participants will complete their homework, on a weekly basis, by the end of the first semester
			By the end of the first semester, 50% of participants will say they understand their math homework better
			By the end of the first semester, tutors will report improvement in 45% of the participants' math skills
			By the end of the school year, 65% of parents will report that their child has an improved attitude toward math
			At the end of the school year, 85% of program participants will pass math

Community assessment findings lead to the designation of the outcome, which, in turn, informs the design of the outcome-based program. The indicators measure how the library program accomplishes the outcome.

DESIGNING THE EVALUATION STRATEGY

Now that the outcome indicators have been designated, it is time to design a strategy for evaluating the effectiveness of each new service or program. The goal here is to select practical evaluation methods that will yield the most useful information possible. To do this, you should ask yourselves the following questions:

- What information is needed to evaluate the success of the program?
- Which data collection methods will yield the most useful findings?
- When should evaluation occur?
- Will program participants be willing and able to participate in the evaluation process?
- Who will conduct the evaluation?

If well written, the indicators themselves will describe the specific information needed to evaluate the success of the program. In our hypothetical scenario, the indicators target percentage rates that, one hopes, will help track accomplishment of the outcome. Therefore, the information needed to evaluate the success of the program includes a baseline population figure (i.e., the number of remedial middle-schoolers participating in the math tutoring program) and, of these, the number of students who actually demonstrate comprehension of their math homework. You will also want to know how many math assignments the kids bring to the tutoring sessions versus how many are actually completed, plus how many of the students end up passing math. Methods for collecting these and other pieces of information are discussed below.

DATA COLLECTION METHODS

There are several ways to measure outcome achievement. Techniques include analyzing outputs; conducting surveys, one-on-one interviews, and focus groups; administering tests; and observation. In developing an evaluation strategy, you must decide which methodologies will yield the most useful information in the most efficient manner. Although most of the methods discussed below were also described as community assessment techniques in chapter 2, it's worth reviewing how they might be used during evaluation.

Analyzing Outputs

Library staff tally many sets of outputs every day. As we have mentioned before, these include library visitors, reference questions, program attendance, circulation of materials, and use of online resources. These statistics document how much your services are used and so play a critical role in the evaluation process. Collecting and analyzing quantitative data to evaluate library service is often far more complicated than just counting numbers, however. In particular, funders and governing bodies will want to know exactly how many people benefited from the library's outcome-based programs. You will, therefore, want to distinguish between overall participation (i.e., total number of users throughout the evaluation period) and unique participants (i.e., counting users only once, regardless of the number of times they participate). Both sets of numbers are important, but they are rarely the same thing, unless you are counting participation in a one-time-only event.

In our case study scenario, we have space for twenty remedial middle school students to participate in the weekly math-tutoring program. Kids register in the fall with the intention of participating during the entire school year. If some drop out, then other wait-listed middle-schoolers can join. Capturing a head count of weekly participation will help you track usage patterns throughout the school year. However, you will also want to record the total number of individual participants—a figure that will exceed the original twenty students as kids cycle in and out of the program. Without a baseline number of individual participants, you will not be able to calculate the percentage of students who actually benefit from the program. Figure 5.2 shows the different ways outputs can be calculated and used as part of the evaluation process.

FIGURE 5.2

Case Study Example: Ways to Count Attendance (i.e., Outputs)
for Weekly Math Tutoring Program

Number of students per week	20
Total program attendance (20 students x 36 school weeks)	720
Total number of individual students who participated in the program	36
Total number of students who attended every week	8

Surveys and Interviews

Although outputs provide important quantitative data, statistics
are just numbers if not considered within the broader context of
outcome-based evaluation. Many libraries use *surveys* to gauge the
success of their programs, possibly because they are easy to administer and tend to yield lots of data in a short period of time. Surveys
also solicit feedback in an anonymous, non-threatening way, which
many respondents appreciate. If well designed, survey questions
generate feedback that can be quickly tabulated and analyzed, especially if done via an online tool, like SurveyMonkey. Plus, surveys
can be administered to many people at once, making them efficient
and cost-effective. Questions may be structured as multiple choice,
open-ended essays, ranked Likert scales, and yes/no or true/false.

On the downside, survey-takers may not understand the questions, because of language barriers or confusing rhetoric. Moreover,
survey instruments are impersonal and non-interactive: participants
are asked to respond to a set of questions, but are never invited to
engage with the evaluator. One way to resolve this is to conduct in-per-
son, one-on-one *interviews,* which are far more personal and effective
at soliciting thoughtful, in-depth responses. Though interview questions are set in advance, answers can be modified or expanded upon
as the conversation progresses. But because of this, interviews are
more time-consuming to administer than written surveys. Furthermore, interviewers must be adept at taking notes quickly and should
be trained how not to bias the conversation. Surveys and interviews
can be used to measure changes in attitude, knowledge, status, or life
condition.

Focus Groups

Focus groups are similar to interviews in that feedback is solicited orally and in person. Where interviews tend to occur between two people, focus groups involve several individuals who share characteristics in common—for example, teenaged mothers, homeless women, sixth-grade boys, midlife adults, or a specific group of people who participated in a particular library program. Here, too, the questions are set in advance, but the group dynamic may take the conversation in unanticipated directions. Ideally, your focus group will consist of 6 to 10 people, who are willing to spend up to an hour talking about the program or service being evaluated. A good facilitator is required to keep the discussion on topic and ensure all participants are heard. Like surveys and interviews, focus groups can be used to measure changes in attitude, knowledge, status, or life condition. But unlike surveys, focus group findings are far more difficult to tabulate and synthesize. Therefore, you should always weigh the benefits of conducting a focus group before bringing people together to solicit their feedback.

Testing and Observation

Testing is the most direct way of measuring an increase in knowledge. The test instrument is administered at the start of the program and then again at the end to see what knowledge was gained. A greater number of correct answers on the post-test provides at least partial evidence of learning. We recommend asking program instructors to create the test instruments because they have subject expertise that library staff might lack. A test might also be used to demonstrate increased skill, if administered before and after the new skill is taught.

Changes in skill can also be measured through *observation*. Success at teaching someone to use an e-book reader, for instance, is measured by observing whether or not the person can now use the device. Observation is an excellent evaluation technique for intentionally studying activities and events as they happen. Observers make note of what they see and then analyze the data to identify patterns and trends. To measure change, pre- and post-observations may be conducted, just as written pre- and post-tests are administered to measure increased knowledge. Observation can be used to evaluate skill levels, changes in behavior, how long it takes to accomplish a task, and how activities change over a period of time.

Triangulation

Regardless of the targeted outcome, you should always try to triangulate results by using two or more evaluation techniques to corroborate findings. Focus groups, for example, might be used to put survey responses into perspective, while observations often provide context to outputs. Triangulation occurs when the findings of your various evaluation techniques complement each other, thus confirming valid and reliable results. However, if findings conflict, then your strategy needs to be revisited. To assist you in designing the most effective plan, we have outlined the advantages and disadvantages of each of the various evaluation techniques in figure 5.3. You will want to use two or more of these methodologies to triangulate successful achievement of your outcome.

OTHER EVALUATION CONSIDERATIONS

When should evaluation occur? Well-written indicators are time-bound and so should help define the evaluation period. For instance, we predict that by the end of the school year, 65 percent of parents will report that their child has a better attitude toward math, as a result of being tutored at the library. To measure this target, you will have to survey or interview the parents at least one or two weeks before school ends. The indicator clearly states the time frame for conducting this part of the evaluation.

Evaluation studies conducted and reported at the end of a program are called "summative," because they sum up what was accomplished over the length of the project. Most libraries engage in summative evaluation, if they evaluate their services at all. However,

FIGURE 5.3

Evaluation Methods: Purpose, Advantages and Challenges

METHOD	OVERALL PURPOSE	ADVANTAGES	CHALLENGES
Analyzing Outputs	Statistical overview of program activity	Doesn't interrupt program or participants; data may already exist; statistics are unbiased	Information may be incomplete; not flexible
Surveys	Quick and/or easy to get lots of information in a non-threatening way	Anonymous, inexpensive to administer; easy to analyze and compare; can administer to many people at once; generates lots of data	May not get careful feedback; wording can bias responses; impersonal; literacy required
Interviews	Solicit respondent's full impressions and experiences and/or learn more about survey responses	Get full range and depth of information; easy to clarify and follow up on responses; literacy not required	Time-consuming; harder to analyze and compare; interviewer can bias responses
Focus Groups	Explore a topic through group discussion	Gather common impressions quickly and reliably; efficient way to compile wide range and depth of information in short time	Harder to analyze; need good facilitator; hard to schedule; may need incentive(s) to motivate participation
Test	Administer exam to assess level of knowledge	Quick and easy way to gauge knowledge level; compare pre- and post-test to measure what was learned	Need subject expert to create instrument; participants may resent having to take a test
Observation	Observe and record activities and events in progress	View activities as they actually occur	May be difficult to interpret what is being observed; presence of observer may influence participant behavior; time-consuming

Adapted from McNamara, C. n.d. Basic guide to program evaluation (including outcomes evaluation). managementhelp.org/evaluation/program-evaluation-guide.htm.

you need not wait till the end of your program to measure its effectiveness. In fact, best practice dictates that evaluation be conducted during service delivery, so modifications can be made as needed. This type of evaluation is called "formative," because it helps keep the program on track and informs any required changes. In our case study scenario, you will want to periodically check with parents, tutors, and students long before the end of the school year to gauge the impact of the tutoring program. If comprehension of math homework isn't occurring, then a program redesign should occur to meet the ultimate outcome. Formative evaluation should be planned and conducted just as thoughtfully as summative evaluation.

You will also want to consider how much data can realistically be collected and analyzed during the life of the outcome-based project. The target population of our hypothetical case study is relatively limited. Soliciting input from small groups is usually manageable, even if done on a formative basis. On the other hand, working with larger audiences, over longer periods of time, is much more challenging. Few libraries today have the resources to adequately synthesize a massive amount of user feedback. For this reason, we encourage starting small by targeting outcome-based services to a very specific and homogeneous population. Once you master the process for a smaller group, you might then try targeting a bigger, more heterogeneous population, but only if you have the resources to conduct a larger-scale evaluation.

Then, of course, there's the question of how willing or able your target population is to participate in the evaluation. Some program participants might be concerned about privacy and/or how much time a survey or focus group will take out of their busy schedules. Language barriers, and lack of technology might preclude others from participating in the evaluation. You will want to make the process as easy as possible, so people can participate. Surveys should be no longer than one page or a single computer screen. Consider using food or gift cards as incentives to attract focus group participants. Remove library jargon from all data collection instruments and conduct surveys, interviews, focus groups, and tests in the target population's native language. Assure everyone that responses will remain confidential and that participation in the evaluation is strictly voluntary. Explain how data results will be used. If the target population understands how important their feedback is to enabling the services they want and need, they may be more willing to participate in the evaluation process.

Lastly, you must decide who will conduct the evaluation. As beneficial as it may be for staff to hear directly from program participants, sometimes it is best to have an objective outsider, like a consultant, conduct the evaluation instead. Staff may know how to count outputs, distribute surveys, and perhaps even run focus groups, but an expert will probably be needed to design the data collection instruments and analyze the results. If you expect to conduct evaluations throughout the life of a year-long program, you may opt to train staff or volunteers on how to collect less complicated data. Rachel Applegate (2013, 159–61) advises not to disregard consultants altogether, however, as their services are often more efficient than that of an inexperienced team. Outside experts also provide a broader context to your project due to their wealth of experience and depth of knowledge. Consultants are often the only ones who can compare your services to other libraries and explain how your results contrast, meet, or exceed the outcomes of similar programs.

IMPLEMENTING THE EVALUATION PLAN: CASE STUDY

Hoping to help remedial middle school students comprehend math assignments, we proposed that the library offer a weekly after-school tutoring program. We also designated several indicators that would help measure achievement of the targeted outcome. Let's see how you would measure accomplishment of these indicators. To help visualize the process, we've provided a basic outline of our strategy in figure 5.4.

FIGURE 5.4

Case Study Example:

Methods for evaluating accomplishment of outcome indicators

COMMUNITY ASSESSMENT FINDINGS	OUTCOME STATEMENT	OUTCOME-BASED LIBRARY PROGRAM	OUTCOME INDICATORS	EVALUATION METHODS
Parents and teachers are concerned that middle school students are failing math	Remedial middle school students comprehend math homework	After-school math tutoring program, offered weekly in the library	At least 60% of program participants will complete their homework, on a weekly basis, by the end of the first semester	Analyze outputs (i.e., number of homework assignments completed)
			By the end of the first semester, 50% of participants will say they understand their math homework better	Survey or interview participating students
			By the end of the first semester, tutors will report improvement in 45% of the participants' math skills	Survey or interview program tutors
			By the end of the school year, 65% of parents will report that their child has an improved attitude toward math	Survey or interview parents of participating students
			At the end of the school year, 85% of program participants will pass math	Analyze outputs (i.e., number of participating students who pass math)

Needed Information

Before proceeding, you must first decide what information is needed to evaluate the success of the program. All of the proposed indicators measure positive change in a percentage of participants. You will, therefore, have to establish how many people actually participate in the program. A weekly head count will be collected as part of your normal output procedures. But because you can't calculate percentages without knowing the exact number of people experiencing positive change, you must also tally individual, unique participants. Part of this will be accomplished by requiring each middle school participant to register. However, to keep an accurate record throughout the year, you will also have to take weekly attendance, especially as less-motivated students start to drop out and wait-listers join.

You will also need the parents' contact information, so you can solicit their feedback by the end of the school year. Asking parents to register their child, in person, is a good way to make initial contact, while requesting their e-mail address and phone number for later use. You may also want to confirm that these are indeed remedial students, by conducting a short pre-test during registration.

Data Collection Methods and When to Use Them

Isolating the variables that lead to academic success can be nearly impossible. Moreover, schools are usually very reluctant to share individual student outcomes. We have set an indicator that 85 percent of program participants will pass math thanks to the library's tutoring program, but the school district may, in fact, refuse to provide this information. That's why we've targeted several achievable and clearly measurable benchmarks to document completion of the outcome. Careful evaluation of the tutoring program can validate the link between library usage and math homework comprehension. Let's see how each of our indicators might be measured.

We have predicted that, by the end of the first semester, 60 percent of program participants will complete their math homework on a weekly basis. This should be relatively easy to assess by asking the tutors to document which students complete their homework during program hours. The overall percentage is then calculated by dividing the number of students who completed their homework by the total number of program participants. For example:

$$\frac{216 \text{ participants completed homework assignments}}{360 \text{ total program participants}} = 60\%$$

In this case, the goal was met, indicating at least partial achievement of your outcome.

We have also predicted that 65 percent of parents will report their child has an improved attitude toward math by the end of the school year. This means, of course, that if you decide to use this indicator, you will have to contact the students' parents to solicit their feedback about the program. You could invite them to participate in a focus group near the end of the academic year; but because you'll be asking questions about individual student performance, a survey or one-on-one interviews would be more private and, therefore, probably more preferable. E-mailing a link to an online survey instrument is both private and convenient. If they don't respond, then you can follow up with a call, since you had the foresight to collect phone numbers, as well as e-mail addresses, during student registration.

We also predicted that, by midyear, 50 percent of program participants will say they understand math better. Moreover, the tutors will report improvement in 45 percent of the students' math skills. Because both the students and their tutors are available on a weekly basis, you should have no trouble either surveying or interviewing them individually about math comprehension and skill retention. If the targets aren't being met, then it's probably time to review the program and make overall adjustments. Measuring these particular targets can also be repeated at the end of the school year to corroborate the results of your other indicators. This will help triangulate your findings and reaffirm that your program is making an impact.

Target Population Willingness and Ability to Participate in the Evaluation

The tutoring program is a year-long initiative that helps kids with their math homework on a weekly basis. Although some students may move in and out of the program, over the length of the school year, the target population is small and relatively easy to monitor. Tracking improvements in comprehension and skills shouldn't be difficult, since participants are an active part of the program and you have several months to follow their progress. Soliciting input from the tutors should also be easy. Gathering parental input may be more complicated, however. Where the kids and their tutors are a captive audience, not so with the parents, who work forty hours a week and lead busy lives. In addition, some might be reluctant to share their e-mail addresses or have little access to technology because of personal circumstances. You could try calling them on the phone for one-on-one interviews, but language barriers might be an issue.

You should also consider getting parental permission before involving children in your evaluation project. Permission slips may be required for any "extraordinary" evaluation activity, such as filmed focus groups. Forms should be sent home well in advance of your first test or survey. You must also assure youngsters and parents alike that all responses will remain anonymous and confidential. Remind them, too, that they all have the right to opt out of testing or any other assessment procedures that make them feel uncomfortable or that they just don't want to do (Dresang, Gross, and Holt 2006, 59).

The Evaluation Team

Your teen librarian is looking forward to overseeing the evaluation of the program's success. She has great rapport with the kids and will supervise the tutors—high school students and education majors from a local college—who provide the weekly homework assistance. But your teen librarian is no math expert, so you enlist the seventh-grade math teacher, who's a member of your OBPE team, to design all interview questions and survey instruments for the project. With his help, the OBPE team will be responsible for analyzing all incoming data and will share results as part of any required formative and summative reports.

Analyzing Results

It is now the end of the academic year. Over the past 10 months, some 36 youngsters participated in the library's weekly tutoring program. Of those, eight students attended regularly throughout the year. Math comprehension was measured via surveys, one-on-one interviews, and homework completion rates. Two "customer satisfaction" surveys were also administered, confirming that most of the kids enjoyed working with the tutors and appreciated being enrolled in the program. Through your contacts at the local middle school, you learn that 22 of the kids (61 percent) who participated in the program passed their math class, including all 8 of the core group of students. Though this falls short of your projected 85 percent, you are thrilled that 100 percent of the regular users accomplished the goal. Furthermore, though you may not be able to show a direct link between the library's program and the kids' improved grades, the tutors are able to corroborate an increase in the middle-schoolers' math skills, indicating that at least part of the outcome was met.

Getting feedback from the parents produced mixed results, however. As suspected, e-mailing the SurveyMonkey link yielded very few responses, so your teen librarian ended up calling most of the parents. Language was a major barrier—many of the parents spoke only Spanish—and people didn't like being bothered at home. So you were unable to collect much data regarding the students' attitude about math. Still, the few responses you did get indicated that kids' attitudes had indeed improved, providing some evidence of success. When planning next year's tutoring program, you will be sure to consider other, more effective ways of soliciting parental feedback, since connecting with them proved so difficult this time around.

THE IMPORTANCE OF EVALUATION

Outcome evaluation measures the impact on, benefits to, and positive changes experienced by community members as a result of participating in the library's services or programs. Without evaluation you may never truly know whether your outcomes have been achieved. By evaluating your programs, you demonstrate to stakeholders that the library is committed to providing the best service possible. If a program isn't productive, you then either modify it or jettison it altogether in favor of more responsive services. Libraries can no longer be everything to everybody—evaluation helps inform service priorities.

Outcome evaluation, in particular, reinforces the relevance of projects that may be small in numbers but big on results. Although only eight middle-schoolers participated regularly in the hypothetical tutoring program, the effort was deemed worthwhile because all eight gained the knowledge needed to understand their homework and pass math. These positive results will no doubt motivate you to provide an even bigger and better program next school year. On the other hand, the lack of parental feedback was disappointing. Obviously, another evaluation strategy will have to be tried if the program is repeated. Your findings will help diagnose the problems that need to be addressed.

Evaluation provides an evidence-based means of communicating achievement to people inside and outside the library. In fact, data collected directly from program participants are often far more politically powerful than other evidence of success or need. If community leaders don't appreciate how you impact people's lives, perhaps it's because the library has done a poor job of evaluating its services. In chapter 6, we explain how to leverage the good work you have accomplished through your outcome-based efforts. Even naysayers have a hard time ignoring the value of the library when the results of a program are confirmed and reported through meticulous evaluation.

REFERENCES

Applegate, Rachel. 2013. *Practical Evaluation Techniques for Librarians.* Santa Barbara, CA: Libraries Unlimited.

Dresang, Eliza T., Melissa Gross, and Leslie Edmonds Holt. 2006. *Dynamic Youth Services through Outcome-Based Planning and Evaluation.* Chicago: American Library Association.

McNamara, Carter. "Basic Guide to Program Evaluation (Including Outcomes Evaluation)." managementhelp.org/evaluation/program-evaluation-guide.htm.

6

Sharing Results

YOU HAVE PUT A LOT OF THOUGHT AND EFFORT INTO planning, implementing, and evaluating a significant library service. Whether you were launching a new initiative or rethinking an older, more established program, you have learned a lot as you worked your way through the OBPE process. You have now reached the final phase. You are ready to share your results with the people who matter, thereby leveraging the library's role in the community.

Mark Gould (2009, vii), the editor of a handbook on public relations for libraries, writes about the needs to grow new audiences and build public support for social change as being reasons for developing effective public awareness campaigns. He urges librarians to unify their communications through a powerful brand, a clear, strong voice, increased visibility, and messages that are amplified through partnership. In this way, we build on library success stories and create support for future initiatives.

You can think of Phase V as a public relations or a communications activity. Certainly it has elements of both. It is also an opportunity to tell your library's story in compelling ways. You now have data to provide to funders or elected officials who are looking for accountability. You have human interest stories to share with the media. Hopefully, you have a successful venture to celebrate with the staff and stakeholders who helped to make it happen. If it was less than successful, you have lessons to learn and share. Most importantly, perhaps, it is a way to continue the conversations you started during Phase I, when you were gathering information from people in your community.

TARGETING YOUR AUDIENCE

Start by listing the various individuals and groups who should know about your results. Here are some ideas to get you started:

- Funders
- Partners
- Library administrators
- Library board or trustees
- Elected officials
- Library staff—those who worked on the project and those who might not be as aware of what you were up to
- Library patrons
- Everyone you talked with during your "gathering information" phase
- The broader library community
- Local media
- Social media

Let's think together about how each target audience might be reached most effectively. We will once again use the example of the three-pronged initiative intended to reach the outcome: "Remedial middle school students comprehend math homework." You started the project at the beginning of the school year and have evaluation data that demonstrates a majority of students participating in the program completed their homework and passed their math class. Two "customer service" surveys confirmed that the kids enjoyed working with the tutors and were grateful for the program. Moreover, the tutors corroborated an increase in the students' math skills. Unfortunately, you weren't able to solicit much feedback from parents, but you have learned from this experience and will rethink this part of the evaluation process before launching next year's program.

Funders

If your project was supported by grant funds, there are almost certainly required protocols for reporting your results. Responding as required and on time will help your credibility if you go back to this source of funding in the future. Library Friends groups and foundations tend to be less formal in their reporting requirements. However, sharing your results with these supporters is particularly important. Hopefully you have kept them informed along the way, perhaps inviting them to an opening event or simply to observe the tutoring program in operation. If you have reached an end point or a milestone—more than half of the participating students completed their math homework and passed their math class—be sure to let them know.

Sometimes a local business will provide funding for homework assistance. They should also be supplied with data, stories, and photos demonstrating the success of the project they have supported. All funders should routinely be acknowledged in any publicity about the service or program they supported. Many libraries provide plaques or labels indicating donors on physical facilities, such as homework centers. Unless your donors have requested anonymity, be generous with your demonstrations of gratitude.

Partners

You probably had some formal partners who helped to make your project a success. For our hypothetical math homework help project, we partnered with the local middle school, the high school, and the education department at the local college. The middle school helped publicize the new math homework services and identified remedial students we could target for participation. The middle school math teacher not only served on the OBPE team, he also designed the evaluation instruments and helped analyze our findings. The high school and college helped us recruit student volunteers. None of these partners received monetary compensation for their services, so the library should be especially generous with its thanks. The library foundation provided a nice reception, where the partners' efforts were acknowledged with plaques they can display in their offices. In addition, each partner received a scrapbook with photos of the program in action and "thank you" notes from the students and parents.

Many librarians have found that successful partnerships reap benefits in ongoing relationships. One Sacramento branch library worked intensively with a local Head Start when they were launching their new Family Space. They discovered that the Head Start staff and parents, having found the library through Family Space, continued to support other programs for children, such as summer reading.

Library Administrators

If you are part of the administrative team, you have no doubt been diligent about reporting the ongoing progress of your OBPE initiative. If, on the other hand, your position is lower in the library hierarchy, you now have the happy task of reporting your success to your superiors. Every library has its own culture and system for such reports. At a minimum, you will want to send them a copy of your final report, along with a brief cover letter thanking them for their support of the project. If appropriate, ask to speak about the initiative at a meeting. You should be aware of their preferences for reporting. Do they want to see an executive summary of the program's results? Would they prefer a PowerPoint presentation? Are they more interested in hard data or in human interest stories? (You should be able to provide both.) Do they value brevity, or do they want to spend some time hearing about the impact of the program on staff, customers, and stakeholders? Tailor your remarks accordingly.

Library Board or Trustees

Although it is customary to wait to be invited to speak to the library board of commissioners or trustees, ordinarily the library director is happy to arrange this. Be sure to honor time constraints and to brief the administration beforehand about the content of your remarks. Board members are notorious for picking up on some tiny detail and running with it. You don't want your boss to be blindsided by some off-the-wall directive arising from your presentation.

Elected Officials

Access to elected officials varies widely. Some local politicians make a point of keeping in close contact with the staff of the government services under their jurisdiction. They like to be able to report to their constituents about the good work being done with their tax dollars, and public libraries are great examples of public value. If this hasn't occurred to your city council member, alderman, or county supervisor, it may be time to raise their awareness. Make friends with their field representatives and begin to bombard them with press releases or informal news notes. Most elected officials are hungry for photo opportunities, so be sure to invite them to events where they can smile at cute children or shake hands with everyday library patrons.

Library Staff

It is surprising how often we fail to keep our own staff informed about the results of the work we do. It is also surprising how often we fail to thank them for the good work they do. Imagine how they would respond to a celebratory staff meeting or special break time at which you share the results of your evaluation. Staff members, who directly help students complete their math homework, had the opportunity to see firsthand the outcomes that were achieved. But they also deserve hearing the formal results of the program and examining both the quantitative and qualitative data. Don't forget the people behind the circulation desk or the support staff who work in the back room and rarely get to see the services firsthand.

Library Patrons

People who use the library after school must have noticed young teenagers working on their homework or huddled over worksheets with a high school student tutor. Let them know the good things that happened as a result. Post your results on the library website and take a tip from the Sacramento Public Library. They printed up cards with statistics that pointed to the need for early literacy services and then showcased their own early childhood services. They also posted statistics from their successful summer reading program on the electronic "silent radio" located above the circulation desk at their central library. You can also reach patrons through more traditional promotional materials, such as bookmarks and postcards. Customize them to reflect your library services and programs.

The Community

This is a perfect time to go back to all of the people you talked to when you were gathering information in Phase I. E-mail, call, drop in for a visit, or send them a written report. They will be pleased to know their feedback paid off in action on the part of the library. Keep a log of these community contacts with phone numbers, e-mail, and current addresses. Jot down when you communicated with them and why.

The Broader Library Community

We may get a little tired of reading those "how I did it good" articles in the library press, but we also appreciate knowing what other libraries are doing to help their communities meet their aspirations as well as their needs. Homework assistance programs are no longer seen as innovative; they are core services in many public libraries now. What is different about the initiative described here is the focus on math. The use of OBPE also makes this a newsworthy story. When you tell your story to professional colleagues, you want to celebrate your success and also be honest about lessons learned. Take the time to write an article for one of the professional journals or deliver a poster session at a state or national conference. This pays off by contributing to the collective knowledge of our profession. It also brings the work of your library to the attention of the broader library community. Some libraries are able to build a national reputation as places where innovative and responsive approaches to community needs are encouraged. This can help when recruiting new staff or approaching new funders. Your accomplishments may also help connect you to a wider network of librarians who are concerned with similar issues.

Local Media

Hopefully you have nurtured contacts with local reporters since gathering the community data in Phase I of your OBPE process. Small neighborhood papers are always looking for photo ops and good local interest stories. If there is a Spanish-language newspaper, radio, or TV outlet in this community, they might be very interested in doing a story on the tutoring program that has provided such a needed service to young teens from Hispanic families. It's often difficult to capture the attention of major newspapers, like the *Los Angeles Times,* in an urban center that generates thousands of stories daily. Even the catastrophic fire at the Los Angeles Public Library's (LAPL's) central library in 1986 was knocked off the front pages when Chernobyl melted down. However, the LAPL got great coverage from the Spanish-language television station for its summer lunch @ the library program in 2015. If your library has a public information office, work with it to be ready to respond to queries from the press. Send press releases at strategic points during your service plans and follow up with phone calls.

Social Media

Social media are ubiquitous now, and many library patrons use one or more services on a regular basis. Writing in *American Libraries,* Ben Bizzle and Maria Flora (2015) remind readers that social media present a cost-effective marketing tool, but shouldn't replace traditional outlets completely. They also point out the need to make your promotional materials memorable so as not to get lost in the clutter of messages that people wade through daily. Bizzle and Flora recommend developing an annual theme for all of a library's marketing. This helps keep the message consistent and recognizable in addition to contributing to the library's brand.

Adding content to your library's web page or Facebook presence should be a routine activity and is an easy way to advertise your services as well as trumpet your success stories. Many California parents, who brought their children to summer meals at the library in 2015, told evaluators that they learned about the program from the library's web page when using the online catalog or looking for other children's programs. You are more likely to reach teens with social media if you involve them in creating the messages and posting them on the outlets most popular in their community. Media tastes change rapidly with this demographic, as do the shorthand forms and codes used on them. Use an outdated emoticon or slang term and you risk losing your young audience.

LEVERAGE

A buzzword we hear a lot these days is "sustainability." It reflects the concern about the fate of a program or service when initial funding runs out. Can the library integrate the new program or service into its ongoing operating budget? Sharing program results strategically can be a way to leverage your successful initiative and ensure its sustainability.

How often have you heard some variant of the tired old expression, "The library is the best-kept secret in town"? Libraries that implement OBPE through all five phases have a powerful weapon to lift that veil of secrecy. They have a new program or service that was generated from actual community concerns and they have a posse of community partners who have shared in the work as well as the results. OBPE libraries have demonstrated outcomes that tell stories about individuals whose lives have been changed by their involvement with the public library. These stories are irresistible when told well—and after all, many of us are passionate storytellers.

Take a few minutes and listen to Pam Sandlian Smith's TED talk (Sandlian Smith 2013). Sandlian Smith is the director of Anythink Libraries in Adams County, Colorado. That catchy new name was part of the rethinking and rebranding done under her watch at that library system. In her talk, she communicates the passion for service to the community that drives the library's innovations. We hear about the boy who asked to use an unused community room to stage a puppet show. He labored there for a week, organizing his puppets, preparing his script, and making posters announcing the event, which ended up being a success. A few weeks later, he returned to the library with his father to say thank you and goodbye. The two had been living in a homeless shelter and were finally moving into an apartment of their own. Thanks to Sandlian Smith, who shared his story, we can imagine what it meant to that boy to have someone say "yes" and let him have the space to dream and create and contribute to his community.

This is really what outcome-based planning and evaluation is all about—another tool for librarians, like Pam Sandlian Smith, who are working wonders on behalf of the people they serve. OBPE expands conversations, so we can put our library resources to work, making our community's dreams and aspirations a reality. Outcome-based planning and evaluation is a way for library heroes to be even more effective advocates for their communities.

REFERENCES

Bizzle, Ben, and Maria Flora. 2015. "Marketing in the Real World." *American Libraries* 46 (May): 46–49.

Gould, Mark R., ed. 2009. *The Library PR Handbook: High-Impact Communications.* Chicago: American Library Association.

Sandlian Smith, Pam. 2013. "What to Expect from Libraries in the 21st Century." Tedxtalks.ted.com/video/What-to-Expect-From -Libraries-i.

APPENDIX A

Community Assessment Environmental Scan: Internal (Library) Factors

Name of Library/Branch:

Date:

FACTORS	FINDINGS	SOURCES
Library history and culture (track record serving specific populations; willingness to offer new services; success in offering new services)		
Service priorities (services offered by the library; mission, goals, and objectives)		
Human assets (number of employees and classifications; staff strengths, interests, languages, diversity, in-house trainers; volunteers)		
Non-human assets (collection; facilities; meeting rooms; workspace; resources to support new projects)		

(Cont.)

FACTORS	FINDINGS	SOURCES
Funding (stability of library's funding; revenue sources; current and past grants)		
Technology infrastructure (age of library's technology; staff comfort with new technology; communication methods)		
Partnerships and library support (relationships with community; Friends; library foundation; consortium memberships)		

Purpose

To provide a snapshot of the library's resources and capacity for implementing new programs or service(s).

Instructions

1. Column #1 (Factors) indicates which aspects to investigate about the library.
2. Record what you find out about each area in column #2 (Findings).
3. Column #3 (Sources) is where you list the sources of information recorded in column #2. Possible sources include the library's strategic plan, annual reports, budget documents, written collection development policies; current and former grants and final reports; written library history; consortial agreements; Friends and/or foundation documents; and the institutional memory of longtime staff.

APPENDIX B

Community Assessment Environmental Scan: External (Community) Factors

Name of Library/Branch:

Date:

FACTORS	FINDINGS	SOURCES
Demographics (ethnicities; languages; educational levels; occupations; income levels; household size)		
Setting (geography; rural vs. urban; climate; rent vs. owned homes)		
Economy (major employers; employment vs. unemployment; growth vs. decline in business)		
Technology (levels of technology community wide; training opportunities)		
Sociocultural (community activities; health statistics; general opportunities)		

(Cont.)

Purpose

To provide a contextual snapshot of the community and the factors that help define it.

Instructions

1. Column #1 (Factors) indicates which community factors to investigate.
2. Record what you find out about each area in column #2 (Findings).
3. Column #3 (Sources) is where you list the sources of information recorded in column #2. Possible sources include demographic databases, such as the census; media articles about the community; chamber of commerce or local school district; and general observations.

APPENDIX C

Community Assessment:
Field Research Questions to Ask Yourself

When conducting a community assessment, the first and easiest field research can be done from your car, bicycle, or bus seat on your way to work. Try taking different routes and pay attention to what you see. Get out of the building and drive or walk around at different times of the day. Ask yourself the following questions:

- How do people get around in your community?
- Is this a suburb with no sidewalks? Or an urban neighborhood where the sidewalks are full of mothers pushing strollers, shoppers pulling wheeled carts, or smartly dressed women wearing sneakers on their way to work?
- Do children and teens get around on bicycles?
- Who rides the bus?
- Where do people shop: "Main Street"? Strip malls? Big-box stores with gigantic parking lots? Farmers markets? Mom-and-pop stores? Shopping centers with acres of parking?
- Where do people congregate: Coffee shops? Shopping malls? Senior citizen centers?
- What do people do for fun? What are some leisure activities people engage in here? And where do they do it?

- How many bars are there? How many churches?
- What languages are used on signs?
- Are businesses opening—or closing?
- What are the employment opportunities in your community? Are there big office buildings? Industrial parks? Healthy small businesses?

APPENDIX D

Community Assessment:
Sample Interview and Focus Group Questions

During your community assessment, you will want to interview partners, key informants, and other representatives of the target population you are hoping to better serve. You can interview people or conduct focus group sessions, depending on the situation. Here's a list of questions to get you started.

For Community Partners

Start with questions that help you get generally acquainted with respondents: "What is your official title?" "How long have you worked at _____?" "How large is the staff there?" Then move on to questions about the community:

1. Tell me what it's like for you to work in this community. From your perspective, what is it like for your clients to live here? What community assets do they rely on? What are their biggest challenges?
2. What is your mission as you work with people here?
3. What are some of the most respected, useful agencies or organizations in this community?
4. What gaps do you see in services and resources?
5. What role should the library play as a community resource for you and the people who live here? What should we do to make the library a more vital part of the community?

6. Is there anybody else I should talk to in order to get a good understanding of this community? Is there anything else I should know?

For Members of the Public

Start with introductions. Tell a little about yourself. Ask participants to say how long they've lived in the community. Follow up with the questions below:

1. What is it like living in this community?
2. What are the most important community organizations or agencies or places for you and your family? Why?
3. What do you like most about living here?
4. What would you change about the community if you could?
5. What kinds of things would have to happen for that change to occur?
6. Is there anything else I should know that would help me make the library a more vital part of the community?

If you are doing a community assessment that targets a particular group—parents, older adults, teens, school age children, non-English-speaking immigrants, and so on—feel free to add a few questions that are more specific, if the general questions don't yield useful information.

Bibliography

Applegate, Rachel. 2013. *Practical Evaluation Techniques for Librarians*. Santa Barbara, CA: Libraries Unlimited.

Bertot, John, Charles R. McClure, and Joe Ryan. 2000. *Statistics and Performance Measures for Public Library Networked Services*. Chicago: American Library Association.

Bizzle, Ben, and Maria Flora. 2015. "Marketing in the Real World." *American Libraries* 46 (May): 46–49.

Braun, Linda. 2014. "Outcomes-Based Futures: Keeping Eyes on the Prize." *American Libraries* 45 (December 18). americanlibrariesmagazine.org/2014/12/18/outcomes-based -futures/.

California Library Association. "California Summer Reading Challenge: Outcomes-Based Summer Reading." calchallenge .org/evaluation/outcomes/.

California State Library. 2014. "Book-to-Action Libraries." www .library.ca.gov/lds/getinvolved/booktoaction//lib_list2014 .html.

California State Library. "Book-to-Action Toolkit." www.library
.ca.gov/lds/getinvolved/booktoaction/.

Cole, Natalie, Virginia Walter, and Eva Mitnick. 2013. "Outcomes +
Outreach: The California Summer Reading Outcomes Initiative."
Public Libraries 52 (March/April). http://publiclibrariesonline
.org/2013/05/outcomes/.

Davis, Denise, and Emily Plagman. 2015. "Project Outcome: Helping
Libraries Capture Their Community Impact." *Public Libraries* 54
(July/August): 33–37.

Dresang, Eliza T., Melissa Gross, and Leslie E. Holt. 2006. *Dynamic
Youth Services through Outcome-Based Planning and Evaluation.*
Chicago: American Library Association.

Durrance, Joan C., and Karen E. Fisher with Marian Bouch Hinton.
2005. *How Libraries and Librarians Help: A Guide to Identifying
User-Centered Outcomes.* Chicago: American Library Association.

Fallows, Deborah. 2015. "A Library of Good Ideas." *The Atlantic,*
August 2. www.theatlantic.com/national/archive/2015/08/
a-library-of-good-ideas/400259/.

Gould, Mark R., ed. 2009. *The Library PR Handbook: High-Impact
Communications.* Chicago: American Library Association.

Hacker, Karen. 2013. *Community-Based Participatory Research.* Los
Angeles: Sage.

Harwood Institute for Public Innovation. 2014. "Libraries
Transforming Communities: LTC Public Innovators Cohort."
www.ala.org/transforminglibraries/libraries-transforming-
communities/cohort.

Institute of Museum and Library Services. "Outcome Based
Evaluations." www.imls.gov/grants/outcome-based
-evaluations.

Klipper, Barbara. 2014. "Making Makerspaces Work for Everyone:
Lessons in Accessibility." *Children and Libraries* 12 (Fall): 5–6.

Koester, Amy. 2014. "Get STEAM Rolling! Demystifying STEAM
and Finding the Right Fit for Your Library." *Children and
Libraries* 12 (Fall): 22–25.

Marcotte, Alison. 2015. "Hartford Public Library Builds, Strengthens Community-Police Relations." *American Libraries* 46 (August 3). americanlibrariesmagazine.org/authors/alison -marcotte/.

McClure, Charles R., David R. Lankes, Melissa Gross, and Beverly Choltco-Devlin. 2002. *Statistics, Measures, and Quality Standards for Assessing Digital Reference Library Services: Guidelines and Procedures.* Syracuse, NY: Information Institute of Syracuse, School of Information Studies, Syracuse University; Tallahassee, FL: School of Information Studies, Information Use Management and Policy Institute, Florida State University. quartz.syr.edu/rdlankes/Publications/Books/Quality.pdf.

McNamara, Carter. "Basic Guide to Outcomes-Based Evaluation for Nonprofit Organizations with Very Limited Resources." manage menthelp.org/evaluation/outcomes-evaluation-guide.htm.

————. "Basic Guide to Program Evaluation (Including Outcomes Evaluation)." managementhelp.org/evaluation/program -evaluation-guide.htm.

"Measuring Program Outcomes: A Practical Approach." (1996). United Way of America. www.nrpa.org/uploadedFiles/nrpa.org/ Professional_Development/Accreditation/COAPRT/Measuring _Program_Outcomes-UW.pdf.

Mediavilla, Cindy. 2001. *Creating the Full-Service Homework Center in Your Library.* Chicago: American Library Association.

Pisarski, Alyssa. 2014. "Finding a Place for the Tween: Makerspaces and Libraries." *Children and Libraries* 12 (Fall): 13–16.

Reitz, Joan M. 2014. "Online Dictionary for Library and Information Science (ODLIS)." www.abc-clio.com/ODLIS/ odlis_A.aspx.

Rubin, Rhea Joyce. 2006. *Demonstrating Results: Using Outcome Measurement in Your Library.* Chicago: American Library Association.

Rudd, Peggy D. "Documenting the Difference: Demonstrating the Value of Libraries through Outcome Measurement." In

Perspectives on Outcome-Based Evaluation for Libraries and Museums, 16–23. Washington DC: Institute of Museum and Library Services. www.imls.gov/assets/1/workflow_staging/AssetManager/perspectivesobe.pdf.

Sandlian Smith, Pam. 2013. "What to Expect from Libraries in the 21st Century." Tedxtalks.ted.com/video/What-to-Expect-From -Libraries-i.

"Santa Monica Public Library Mission and Vision." smpl/org/Mission_and_Vision.aspx.

"Santa Monica Public Library Policies." smpl.org/policies.aspx.

Stringer, Ernest T. 2014. *Action Research.* 4th ed. Los Angeles: Sage.

Teasdale, Rebecca. 2015. "Project Outcome Launch—Seven Surveys to Measure Impact." *Public Libraries Online* (May 28). publiclibrariesonline.org/2015/05/project-outcome-launch -seven-surveys-to-measure-impact/.

Van House, Nancy, and Douglas Zweizig, 1987. *Output Measures for Public Libraries: A Manual of Standardized Procedures.* Chicago: American Library Association.

Walter, Virginia A. 1995. *Output Measures and More: Planning and Evaluating Public Library Services for Young Adults.* Chicago: American Library Association.

———. 1992. *Output Measures for Public Library Service to Children: A Manual of Standardized Procedures.* Chicago: American Library Association.

Walter, Virginia A., and Cindy Mediavilla. 2003. "Homework Center Outcomes." UCLA Department of Information Studies. is-intranet.gseis.ucla.edu/research/homework/.

Walter, Virginia A., and Elaine Meyers. 2003. *Teens & Libraries: Getting It Right.* Chicago: American Library Association.

Weak, Emily. 2014. "Simple Steps to Starting a Seed Library." *Public Libraries* 53 (July/August): 24–26.

Williment, Kenneth. 2011. "It Takes a Community to Create a Library." *Public Libraries* 50 (March/April): 30–35.

Working Together Project. 2008. "Community-Led Libraries Toolkit." Vancouver, Canada. www.librariesincommunities.ca/resources/Community-Led_Libraries_Toolkit.pdf.

Zweizig, Douglas, and Eleanor Jo Rodger. 1982. *Output Measures for Public Libraries: A Manual of Standardized Procedures.* Chicago: American Library Association.

About the Authors

MELISSA GROSS is professor and doctoral program chair in the School of Information Studies at Florida State University and past president of the Association for Library and Information Science Education. She received her PhD from the University of California, Los Angeles, in 1998 and was awarded the prestigious American Association of University Women Recognition Award for Emerging Scholars in 2001. Gross has published extensively in the areas of information-seeking behavior, information literacy, library program and service evaluation, information resources for youth, and teacher/librarian collaboration.

CINDY MEDIAVILLA is a lecturer for the UCLA Department of Information Studies. She is also a freelance consultant, who has evaluated and managed several grant-funded projects for public libraries throughout southern California, and is a popular workshop trainer. Mediavilla is best known for her work on after-school homework programs and is the author of *Creating the Full-Service Homework Center in Your Library* (2001). Her master's degree and doctorate in library science are both from UCLA.

VIRGINIA A. WALTER has retired from her work as a full-time tenured professor at the UCLA Department of Information Studies. However, she continues to teach classes and advise students at UCLA and is an active library consultant and trainer, who has been invited to speak at many domestic and international venues. She is the author of many journal articles, nine monographs, and two books for young people. She has an MLS from UC Berkeley and a PhD in public administration from the University of Southern California. Walter is a past president of the Association for Library Service to Children.

Index